PENGUIN BOOKS

D0715974

Dessert

BIBLE

Dessert

BIBLE

Introduction

What meal is complete without a sweet finale? There's nothing like a home-made delight to put a smile of satisfaction on everyone's face.

The possibilities for indulging your sweet tooth are endless, with an infinite variety of desserts to choose from. Fruit salads, trifles and sorbets are refreshing in summer, while puddings, pies and crumbles are perfect for warming up in winter. Quick treats like loganberry sago make an effortless follow-up to a weeknight family dinner, while more elaborate delicacies like individual lemon soufflés are great for a classy dinner party.

But don't think just because the desserts in this book look and taste fantastic that it means they're difficult to make. Most of these recipes are fast and easy to prepare, and many can be made in advance. The hardest part is deciding which one to try first!

Hints for making delicious desserts

- Whichever dessert you are making, preparation is important. Use good quality ingredients and pay attention to measurements.

- For cakes and tarts, make sure you have a suitable baking tin. Grease, line with non-stick baking paper, or dust with flour, before preparing the cake mixture. If this is not done properly the cooked cake will stick to the tin and break up when you try to turn it out.

- Measure all ingredients first, before beginning the method.

- When baking, preheat the oven to the correct temperature. Cake mixtures should be baked immediately to give the best results.

- Use butter and oil at room temperature unless otherwise specified.

- Use large eggs, at room temperature, unless otherwise specified.

- Use full-cream milk unless otherwise specified.

- Always sift flour before use to remove lumps and incorporate air into your mixture.

How to...

BEAT: mix vigorously with a spoon or electric mixer.

BLEND: combine one ingredient with another until completely mixed together; either using a wooden spoon or electric mixer.

STIR: mix carefully in a circular motion to combine.

CREAM: mix butter or oil, alone or mixed with sugar, until light, pale yellow and fluffy.

FOLD: carefully incorporate one mixture into another — usually a light one such as whipped egg whites into a heavier mixture. Folding involves gently 'drawing' a figure of eight with a metal spoon and being careful not to knock the air out of the lighter mixture.

WHIP: beat rapidly with a whisk or electric mixer to incorporate as much air as possible. Cream or egg whites are examples of ingredients that are whipped.

COOK IN A BAIN-MARIE (WATER BATH): place the baking tin or mould into a baking dish, and pour boiling water into the dish until it reaches halfway up the sides of the tin or mould. Then bake the dessert for the stated time. This method is suitable for delicate mixtures that require a gentle, indirect heat — e.g. custards, puddings and soufflés.

BAKE BLIND: precook pastry by lining it with non-stick baking paper, weighing it down with uncooked rice, dried pulses or pastry weights and baking it in the oven.

MELT CHOCOLATE: microwave or use a double boiler. To microwave, place chopped chocolate into a microwave-safe bowl and heat on MEDIUM until partially melted. Remove and stir until melted and smooth. To use a double boiler, place chopped chocolate into a double boiler and stir over simmering water until melted and smooth. Alternatively, place chocolate into a metal bowl and stir over a saucepan of simmering water until melted (the water should not touch the base of the bowl). Be careful not to let any water get into the chocolate.

Amaretto zabaglione

3 egg yolks

2 tablespoons white sugar

2 tablespoons Amaretto liqueur

Place all ingredients into a medium saucepan. Use a hand-held electric mixer on high speed to beat until foamy. Continue beating over a medium heat. The zabaglione will thicken and increase in volume significantly. Once warmed through, remove from the heat.

Continue beating, returning the saucepan to the heat at regular intervals, then removing quickly each time the mixture has warmed through. Be careful not to overheat or the mixture will curdle.

The zabaglione is ready when it is foaming, thick, tripled in volume and warmed through (but not hot).

Can be served warm or chilled.

Serve with fresh fruit or with sweet biscuits crumbled on top.

SERVES 4

Apple and cherry tart

1 tablespoon butter

4 cooking apples, peeled,
  cored and diced

⅓ cup white sugar

1 teaspoon ground cinnamon

1 teaspoon ground allspice

1 teaspoon freshly squeezed
  lemon juice

1 tablespoon plain flour

150 g cherries, fresh or tinned
  (drained)

1 large sheet shortcrust pastry

1 egg yolk

1 tablespoon milk

Preheat oven to 180°C. Grease and flour a baking tray.

Melt butter in a saucepan, then add apples, sugar, spices and lemon
juice. Cover and simmer for 5 minutes. Take off the heat and let cool
5 minutes, then stir in sifted flour and cherries. Set aside to cool.

Cut pastry into a circle and transfer to the baking tray. Spoon apple and
cherry mixture into the centre of the pastry, leaving a 4-cm border around
the edge. Fold the excess pastry over the filling towards the middle,
pleating the edges to create a rim. Whisk the egg yolk and milk together
and brush over the pastry rim.

Bake for 35 minutes, or until pastry is golden-brown.

SERVES 8

Apple cake with caramel sauce

CAKE

2¾ cups plain flour

1 teaspoon bicarbonate of soda

2 teaspoons ground cinnamon

1 teaspoon salt

500 g golden delicious apples,
  peeled, cored, and diced

½ cup soft brown sugar,
  firmly packed

½ cup white sugar

1 cup apple sauce

½ cup vegetable oil

3 eggs

2 teaspoons vanilla extract

SAUCE

115 g unsalted butter

1 cup soft brown sugar,
  firmly packed

¼ cup milk

2 teaspoons vanilla extract

Preheat oven to 180°C. Grease and flour a 12-cup Bundt tin.

For cake, sift together flour, baking soda, cinnamon and salt. In a separate bowl, toss apples with 2–3 tablespoons of the flour mixture.

In another bowl, combine the sugars, apple sauce, oil, eggs and vanilla. Beat for about 5 minutes, until mixture is thick. Gradually beat in remaining flour mixture. Fold in apples.

Pour mixture into prepared tin. Bake for about 1 hour, or until a skewer inserted comes out clean. Cool in the tin on a wire rack. >

For caramel sauce, melt butter in a heavy-based saucepan. Mix in brown sugar, then milk. Stir for about 5 minutes, until boiling. Add vanilla.

While still hot, spoon a quarter of the sauce over the warm cake in the tin. Leave for 10 minutes to soak in. Let cake cool at least 1 hour before serving – as it cools, continue spooning over remaining sauce now and then. This will form a nice glaze.

SERVES 12

Apple crumble with coriander

6 apples, peeled, cored and sliced

2 teaspoons ground cinnamon

1 teaspoon ground nutmeg

1 cup plain flour

2 teaspoons ground coriander

½ cup white sugar

125 g cold butter, cut into small pieces

Preheat oven to 180°C and grease a baking dish.

Layer the apple slices in the baking dish. Sprinkle over cinnamon and nutmeg.

Sift flour and ground coriander into a bowl, add sugar and mix well. Rub butter into dry ingredients until mixture resembles breadcrumbs.

Spoon the crumble mixture evenly over the apples. Bake for 30 minutes or until top is golden-brown.

Serve with cream or ice-cream.

SERVES 4–6

Apricot and almond pudding

175 g softened unsalted butter

175 g castor sugar

175 g ground almonds

3 eggs, separated

1 teaspoon vanilla extract

8 apricot halves (tinned or fresh)

Preheat oven to 150°C. Grease a shallow 20-cm baking dish.

Cream the butter with the sugar, then add the ground almonds and mix well. Add the beaten egg yolks and vanilla.

In a separate bowl, whisk the egg whites until stiff, then fold into the almond mixture.

Spoon into the prepared dish and place apricot halves (flat-side down) on top.

Bake for 30 minutes, then turn oven temperature up to 180°C. Cook for a further 20–30 minutes or until the top is golden and a skewer inserted into the middle comes out clean.

Serve warm with ice-cream.

SERVES 6

Apricot hazelnut bites

500 g finely ground hazelnuts

1½ cups castor sugar

1 teaspoon vanilla extract

3 egg whites

½-cup apricot jam

icing sugar, to serve

Preheat oven to 180°C. Grease and flour two baking trays.

Combine ground hazelnuts, sugar and vanilla in a bowl.

In a separate bowl, whip egg whites until soft peaks form. Gently fold in hazelnut mixture to form a paste.

Roll a tablespoon of mixture into a ball that measures 2–3 cm across. Make a small hole in the centre and fill with a teaspoon of jam. Cover the hole with a little more mixture, and roll in your hands to seal. Place onto prepared tray. Repeat with remaining mixture and jam.

Bake for 20–25 minutes, until light golden. Cool on a wire rack.

Dust with icing sugar to serve.

MAKES 30

Autumn fruits in spiced wine

300 ml red wine

1 cinnamon stick

3 cloves

2–3 whole allspice

1 star anise

½ teaspoon ground nutmeg

½ cup soft brown sugar

zest of ½ an orange,
    thinly sliced

4 plums, stoned and sliced

2 pears, stoned and sliced

200 g fresh blackberries
    or raspberries

Combine wine, cinnamon, cloves, allspice, star anise, nutmeg, sugar and orange zest in a saucepan. Stir over a low heat, without simmering, for 5–10 minutes. Add fruit and heat, without simmering, until fruit is just tender.

Serve warm, with double cream. (You can also leave to steep for several hours at room temperature, to allow flavours to fully develop. Simply warm through before serving.)

SERVES 4–6

Baked apples with chocolate sauce

4 apples

4 figs, chopped

120 g camembert, chopped
into small pieces

1 cup chopped walnuts

4 tablespoons honey

2 tablespoons freshly squeezed
lemon juice

SAUCE

2 tablespoons honey

⅓ cup cocoa

⅓ cup water

2 tablespoons double cream

Preheat oven to 200°C.

Core apples using an apple corer. Use a melon baller to scoop out the inside of each apple. Leave about a 1.5-cm wall. Reserve flesh. Cook hollowed-out apples for a few minutes in the microwave, until soft.

Mix reserved apple flesh with all filling ingredients. Stuff apples with filling and place on a baking tray. Bake about 5 minutes, until hot and cheese has melted.

For the chocolate sauce, heat the honey, cocoa and water in a saucepan. Once hot, stir in cream and simmer until thickened.

Pour sauce over baked apples and serve hot, with cream or ice-cream.

SERVES 4

Baked custard

600 ml milk

3 tablespoons honey

3 eggs

pinch of salt

Preheat oven to 180°C and grease six ½-cup ramekins.

Heat the milk until almost boiling, then stir in honey. In a bowl, beat the eggs and salt. Slowly add the hot milk to the eggs and mix until combined.

Pour mixture into ramekins and bake in a bain-marie (see page ix) for 30 minutes or until firm.

Cool to room temperature, then chill in the refrigerator. Serve cold with fresh or stewed fruit.

SERVES 6

Baklava

SYRUP

2 cups white sugar

1 cup honey

1½ cups water

1 tablespoon freshly squeezed
  lemon juice

1 teaspoon ground cinnamon

FILLING

2 cups finely chopped walnuts

1 cup finely chopped almonds

1 teaspoon ground cinnamon

¼ cup soft brown sugar

50 g butter

30 sheets filo pastry

200 g butter, melted

Preheat oven to 160°C. Grease a 20-cm × 30-cm cake tin.

For syrup, combine sugar, honey, water, lemon juice and cinnamon over low heat. Stir until sugar dissolves. Increase heat and simmer for about 5 minutes, until the mixture is syrupy. Remove from heat and set aside to cool.

For filling, blend all ingredients in a food processor.

To assemble, place a sheet of filo into the bottom of the prepared cake tin and brush with melted butter. (Keep remaining filo covered with a damp tea towel so it doesn't dry out.) One at a time, place another ten sheets of filo on top of the first, brushing each sheet with melted butter before adding the next. Spread over half of the filling mixture. Top with 10 more filo sheets, brushing each with butter. Spread over remaining filling mixture, then top with remaining pastry sheets, brushing each with butter.

Use a sharp knife to cut the baklava into diamond shapes in the tin. Bake for 1 hour, or until golden. Let stand 5 minutes, then pour syrup evenly over the top. Let stand at room temperature 6 hours before serving. Do not refrigerate – store in an airtight container at room temperature.

Serve as an accompaniment to coffee.

SERVES 12

Baltic bubert with stewed fruit

6 heaped teaspoons white sugar

3 heaped teaspoons plain flour

3 eggs, separated

1 teaspoon vanilla extract
(or 1 teaspoon finely grated
lemon zest)

600 ml milk

¼ cup dried apple, chopped

¼ cup dried apricots, chopped

¼ cup dried pears, chopped

¼ cup prunes, chopped

1 tablespoon raisins

2 cloves

2 tablespoons white sugar

1 teaspoon cornflour (optional)

For bubert, mix together sugar, sifted flour, egg yolks and vanilla until well combined. Add enough milk to the mixture to create a runny consistency.

Boil remaining milk in a saucepan. Add egg mixture while stirring constantly. Return to the boil then remove from the heat. Beat egg whites until peaks form. Gently fold into milk mixture.

For stewed fruit, place all ingredients into a saucepan and just cover with water. Boil until fruit is soft. Add cornflour to thicken if desired.

Serve bubert at room temperature (do not refrigerate) with warm stewed fruit on the side.

SERVES 4–6

Banana parfait

500 ml thickened cream

1 teaspoon vanilla extract

1 teaspoon soft brown sugar

⅓ cup castor sugar

250 ml cold crème fraîche

3 bananas

2 cups crumbled shortbread biscuits

2 tablespoons shredded coconut

In a heavy-based saucepan, combine cream, vanilla, brown sugar and 2 tablespoons of the castor sugar. Simmer for 20 minutes. Pour into a bowl and chill for at least 4 hours (or overnight), until cold.

In a separate bowl, beat together crème fraîche and remaining castor sugar until thick and fluffy. Remove vanilla cream from the refrigerator and whisk until smooth.

Peel bananas and cut diagonally into 1-cm slices. Spoon the vanilla cream into six pretty serving glasses or bowls. Top with half the banana slices and sprinkle with three-quarters of the crumbled shortbread. Spoon over crème fraîche and top with remaining banana slices. Sprinkle over remaining shortbread crumbs and coconut and serve immediately.

SERVES 6

Barbecued chocolate bananas

4 bananas, skin on

1 × 150-g block milk chocolate, chopped

Make a slit along the length of each banana. Insert chunks of chocolate into the slits.

Cook on the barbecue until the skins have blackened and chocolate has melted.

Serve immediately.

Berries in jelly

2½ cups mixed berries, fresh or frozen (defrosted)
2 packets strawberry or raspberry jelly

Cover base of eight 1-cup moulds with half the berries. Make jelly according to the directions on the packet. Pour enough jelly into each mould to just cover the berries. Refrigerate 15 minutes, or until starting to set.

Divide remaining berries between the moulds, and cover with remaining jelly. Refrigerate until set.

Unmould onto individual serving plates to serve.

SERVES 8

Berry granita

½ cup white sugar

½ cup water

500 g mixed berries — strawberries (hulled),
blackberries, raspberries

2 tablespoons freshly squeezed lemon juice

Chill a metal baking tray in the freezer.

Stir sugar and water over low heat until sugar has dissolved. Then bring
to the boil and simmer for 5 minutes. Set aside to cool.

Purée berries and lemon juice in a blender until smooth. Add sugar syrup
and blend until smooth.

Using a plastic sieve, strain the berry purée to remove seeds. Pour mixture
into chilled tray and freeze for 2 hours, or until just frozen around the
edges. Use a fork to scrap the granita into ice crystals. Return to the
freezer for 1 hour then stir again. Repeat until the mixture is a smooth,
light consistency.

Before serving, soften a little in the fridge and stir, then refreeze briefly.

SERVES 4–6

Berry surprise pie

500 g frozen puff pastry

700 g berries, fresh or frozen (defrosted)

1 egg

castor sugar, for sprinkling

Preheat oven to 200°C and grease a baking tray.

Roll out the puff pastry on a floured surface to make a 30-cm round and transfer to the baking tray.

Pile the berries into the centre of the pastry, leaving a handful aside for decoration. Beat the egg with a little water and brush the outer rim of the pastry.

Bring the pastry edge towards the middle, leaving a hole in the centre. Pleat and fold the pastry over the fruit to create a rim. Brush top of the pastry with the rest of the egg mix and sprinkle with castor sugar.

Bake for 30 minutes or until the pastry is puffed and golden.

Sprinkle the reserved berries over the top and serve warm with cream or ice-cream.

SERVES 6

Black and white bread pudding with Bailey's sauce

2 cups cream

⅓ cup Bailey's Irish Cream

¼ cup white sugar

½ teaspoon vanilla extract

2 teaspoons cornflour

2 teaspoons water

350 g baguette, cut into
2-cm cubes

170 g dark cooking chocolate,
chopped

170 g white chocolate, chopped

4 eggs

¾ cup white sugar

2 teaspoons vanilla extract

½ cup milk

2 cups cream

To make the sauce, combine cream, Bailey's, sugar and vanilla in a heavy saucepan. Bring to the boil, stirring frequently. Mix together sifted cornflour and water, then whisk into the cream mixture. Boil, stirring constantly, for about another 3 minutes, or until the sauce thickens. Set aside to cool, then refrigerate until cold.

For the pudding, put the bread and chocolate into a large bowl. In a separate bowl, beat together the eggs, 2 tablespoons of the sugar and vanilla. Gradually beat in milk and 1½ cups of the cream. Stir into the bread and chocolate mixture. Let stand for 30 minutes.

Preheat oven to 180°C. Grease a 33-cm × 23-cm baking dish.

Put mixture into baking dish. Pour over remaining cream and sprinkle with remaining sugar. Bake for about 1 hour, until edges are golden and custard is set.

Serve warm with Bailey's sauce.

SERVES 8

Blackberry and nectarine sundaes

250 g fresh blackberries

1 tablespoon icing sugar

2 tablespoons Chambord (or other berry liqueur)

5 nectarines, stoned and sliced

½ cup toasted pecans

1 litre vanilla ice-cream

Purée blackberries in a food processor, then strain through a plastic sieve into a bowl to remove seeds. Stir in sugar and liqueur.

Spoon some of the blackberry sauce into six individual sundae dishes. Spoon over half the nectarine pieces and pecans, then add two scoops of ice-cream to each dish. Top with more blackberry sauce and remaining nectarine pieces.

Sprinkle with remaining pecans to serve.

SERVES 6

Black forest cake

CAKE

1¼ cups self-raising flour

⅓ cup cocoa

½ teaspoon bicarbonate of soda

¾ cup soft brown sugar

75 g butter

¾ cup hot water

2 egg whites

FILLING

250 g ricotta

1 tablespoon icing sugar

1 teaspoon vanilla extract

250 g tinned pitted black
    cherries, drained

icing sugar, to serve

Preheat oven to 180°C. Lightly grease a 23-cm ring tin and line the base.

For cake, sift together the flour, cocoa and bicarbonate of soda. In a separate bowl, combine sugar, butter and hot water. Add flour mixture to sugar mixture and beat well. Add egg whites and beat until well combined.

Pour mixture into prepared tin and bake for 30 minutes, or until a skewer inserted comes out clean. Cool in the tin on a wire rack for 5 minutes before turning out onto the rack to cool completely.

For filling, beat together ricotta, sifted icing sugar and vanilla until smooth.

Use a long bread knife to slice the cake in half horizontally. Place the bottom cake layer onto a serving plate and spread with the filling. Scatter over the cherries, reserving a handful for decoration. Place remaining cake half on top of the filling.

To serve, dust with icing sugar and decorate with remaining cherries.

SERVES 6−8

Blueberry pancakes

2 eggs

½ cup milk

¼ cup castor sugar

1 teaspoon vanilla extract

1 cup self-raising flour

2 cups frozen blueberries (defrosted)

butter, for frying

Whisk together eggs, milk, sugar, vanilla and sifted flour, then stir in the blueberries. Transfer batter to a jug for easy pouring.

Heat some butter in a frying pan until it is foaming, then add about a quarter of a cup of batter to the pan. Depending on the size of your pan, you may have room for three or four pancakes at a time.

Cook pancakes for about 2 minutes or until bubbles appear on the surface. Flip over and cook on the other side for about a minute, until golden.

Stack pancakes on a plate and keep warm while you finish cooking the rest of the batter.

Serve warm with maple syrup.

SERVES 6

Blueberry pudding

¾ cup castor sugar

¼ cup water

1 tablespoon freshly squeezed
   lemon juice

1 teaspoon cornflour

300 g blueberries

1 cup plain flour

2 teaspoons baking powder

1 teaspoon salt

1 egg

½ cup milk

120 g unsalted butter,
   melted and cooled

1 teaspoon vanilla extract

Preheat oven to 190°C and grease a 23-cm square baking dish.

Put ¼ cup of the sugar, plus water, lemon juice and sifted cornflour into
a small saucepan and mix. Stir in blueberries, then simmer for 3 minutes,
stirring occasionally. Set aside.

In a bowl, sift together flour, baking powder and salt. Add remaining sugar.
In a separate bowl, whisk together egg, milk, butter and vanilla. Add flour
mixture and mix until just combined.

Spoon this mixture into prepared dish, then pour over blueberry mixture.
Bake for 25–30 minutes, or until a skewer inserted comes out clean.
Cool in the baking dish on a wire rack for 5 minutes before serving.

SERVES 6–8

Brandy truffles

2 × 375-ml tins evaporated milk

185 g dark cooking chocolate, chopped

2½ cups plain sweet biscuits, crushed

½ cup icing sugar

250 g walnuts, chopped

⅓ cup brandy

chocolate sprinkles or icing sugar, for coating

Stir evaporated milk and chocolate over low heat until chocolate has melted and mixture has thickened. Add biscuit crumbs, sugar, walnuts and brandy and mix until well combined.

Set aside to cool for 30 minutes.

Shape teaspoonfuls of the mixture into balls, then roll in sprinkles or icing sugar to coat.

Refrigerate until ready to serve.

MAKES 70

Bread pudding

½ cup raisins

1 loaf stale sliced white bread

60 g butter

1 cup white sugar

3 eggs, beaten

1 cup milk

1 cup cream

2 teaspoons vanilla extract

1 teaspoon ground cinnamon

icing sugar, to serve

Soak raisins in a bowl of hot water for 20 minutes.

Preheat oven to 180°C and grease a 1-litre casserole dish.

Butter bread slices on both sides. Toast on baking trays in the oven, lightly browning both sides. Allow to cool, then cut into pieces.

Mix together sugar, eggs, milk, cream, vanilla and cinnamon. Drain raisins.

Arrange toast pieces in the casserole dish. Add raisins and pour over egg mixture. Stir so that bread is coated with mixture.

Bake for 40 minutes. Serve hot, dusted with icing sugar.

SERVES 6

Caramel cheesecake

1 × 250-g packet butternut snap
   biscuits, finely crushed

2 tablespoons soft brown sugar,
   firmly packed

100 g unsalted butter, melted

900 g cream cheese, at room
   temperature

1 cup soft brown sugar,
   firmly packed

35 g butter, melted

5 eggs

1 teaspoon vanilla extract

1½ cups white sugar

¼ cup water

1 cup cream

160 g dark chocolate, grated

Preheat oven to 180°C and grease a 23-cm springform tin.

For base, mix together crushed biscuits, sugar and butter. Press mixture firmly into base of prepared tin. Wrap outside of the tin in three layers of foil. Bake for 10–15 minutes, until firm. Cool.

For filling, beat cream cheese and sugar until smooth. Beat in butter, then add eggs one at a time, beating after each addition until just blended. Beat in vanilla.

Pour filling into tin. Bake in a bain-marie (see page ix) for 60–70 minutes, until edges have puffed up but centre is not completely set. Chill in the refrigerator overnight.

For topping, combine sugar and water in a saucepan. Stir over a medium heat until sugar has dissolved, then bring to the boil. Boil for about 10 minutes, without stirring, until mixture turns a rich golden colour. Add cream and reduce heat. Simmer for 8 minutes. Chill topping for 15 minutes, until thickened but not set.

Pour caramel over the top of the cake and decorate with grated chocolate. Chill for at least 2 hours (and up to 6 hours) before serving.

SERVES 14–16

Carrot and walnut puddings

1½ cups self-raising flour

1½ teaspoons baking powder

¾ cup vegetable oil

2 carrots, grated

1 cup soft brown sugar

3 eggs

1 teaspoon vanilla extract

1 teaspoon ground cinnamon

150 g toasted walnuts, chopped

Preheat oven to 180°C. Grease six 1-cup ramekins.

Beat together all ingredients (except nuts) until well combined.
Stir in nuts.

Spoon mixture into ramekins and cover each loosely with foil.

Bake in a bain-marie (see page ix) for 35 minutes. Cool in ramekins
on a wire rack for 5 minutes.

Unmould onto individual serving plates and serve with whipped cream
flavoured with a little grated lemon zest and vanilla extract.

SERVES 6

Chai-spiced rice pudding

3 cups milk

2 cups coconut milk

1 cup arborio rice

½ cup white sugar

¼ teaspoon salt

1 tablespoon grated fresh ginger

½ cup raisins

1 teaspoon ground cinnamon

1 teaspoon ground cardamom

½ teaspoon ground allspice

Combine milk, coconut milk, rice, sugar and salt in a heavy-based saucepan. Bring to the boil over a high heat, stirring continuously. Add ginger and raisins. Reduce heat and simmer for about 40 minutes, stirring frequently, until pudding is thick and rice is cooked. Mix in spices.

Serve warm with cream.

SERVES 6

Cherry chocolate panettone cake

CAKE

1 large panettone

100 g dark cooking chocolate, chopped

425 g tinned pitted black cherries, drained (reserve syrup)

1 cup milk

1 cup cream

4 eggs

1 teaspoon vanilla extract

¼ cup castor sugar

SAUCE

reserved cherry syrup

¾ cup water

⅓ cup kirsch or other brandy

⅓ cup castor sugar

Preheat oven to 180°C. Grease a 20-cm springform tin and place in a large roasting dish (this will catch any liquid that leaks out during cooking).

For cake, cut panettone into thick slices. Cover the base of the tin with a layer of panettone, then top with a layer of cherries and chocolate pieces. Repeat layers until all ingredients are used up, finishing with a layer of chocolate and cherries. >

In a bowl, whish together milk, cream, eggs, vanilla and sugar. Pour mixture over panettone and set aside for 10 minutes to allow liquid to soak in.

Bake for 45 minutes or until a skewer inserted comes out clean.

For sauce, gently heat reserved cherry syrup, water, kirsch and sugar until sugar dissolves. Bring to the boil and heat without stirring until sauce thickens. (Swirl saucepan occasionally.)

Serve hot, drizzled with cherry sauce.

SERVES 8

Cherry clafoutis

800 g tinned pitted cherries,
   well drained
½ cup plain flour
pinch of salt
⅓ cup white sugar

4 eggs
1 teaspoon vanilla extract
1 cup milk
1 tablespoon butter, melted
icing sugar, to serve

Preheat oven to 180°C. Grease a 23-cm shallow pie dish.

Spread cherries in a single layer over the pie dish.

Combine sifted flour, salt and sugar in a bowl. In a separate bowl mix the eggs, vanilla, milk and butter. Make a well in the centre of the dry ingredients and gradually add the egg mixture. Beat until smooth.

Pour mixture over cherries. Bake for 30 minutes or until risen and golden-brown.

Dust with icing sugar and serve hot.

SERVES 6

Choc-chip custard ice-cream

150 g dark chocolate, chopped

400 ml custard

1¼ cups cream

100 g chocolate chips

NOTE: This recipe requires an ice-cream maker.

Melt chocolate (see page x). Set aside to cool a little, then stir in custard and cream until well combined. Stir in choc chips.

Pour the mixture into an ice-cream maker and freeze according to the machine's instructions.

SERVES 6

Chocolate and strawberry trifle

500 g strawberries, hulled and halved

¼ cup icing sugar

600 g chocolate cake, broken into pieces

2 cups thickened cream, whipped

200 g milk chocolate, grated

extra strawberries, to serve

Toss strawberries with sifted icing sugar. Cover bottom of a trifle dish or individual glasses with a layer of cake pieces. Scatter over a third of the strawberries, then spoon over a layer of cream. Sprinkle with grated chocolate. Repeat with two more layers of cake, strawberries, cream and grated chocolate. Chill for at least 2 hours before serving.

To serve, garnish with strawberries and a little more grated chocolate.

SERVES 6

Chocolate baked alaska

3 chocolate muffins

6 large scoops chocolate ice-cream

12 egg whites

600 g castor sugar

Slice the top off the muffins, to create a flat surface. Then cut each muffin in half horizontally. Lay the muffin slices out on a baking tray. Place a scoop of chocolate ice-cream on top of each muffin slice. Store in the freezer while you make the meringue.

Whisk the egg whites until soft peaks form. Continue whisking as you gradually add the sugar. Whisk until the meringue forms thick glossy peaks.

Remove muffin bases from the freezer and cover each with meringue.

Brown the meringue under a very hot grill for a few seconds (or use a mini blowtorch), until golden.

Serve immediately.

SERVES 6

Chocolate berry croissant cake

6 stale croissants, sliced

2 stale pain au chocolat
(chocolate croissants), sliced

½ cup blueberries, fresh or
frozen (defrosted)

½ cup raspberries, fresh or
frozen (defrosted)

½ cup ground almonds

3 eggs

1 cup milk

½ cup cream

½ teaspoon vanilla extract

¾ cup castor sugar

⅓ cup flaked almonds

Preheat oven to 160°C. Lightly grease a 20-cm springform tin.

Cover base of tin with a layer of plain croissant slices. Sprinkle over some of the berries and ground almonds. Top with a layer of croissant and pain au chocolat slices, then more berries and ground almonds. Repeat layering of breads, berries and almonds until all are used. Press down firmly.

Beat together eggs, milk, cream, vanilla and sugar. Pour over cake and set aside for 30 minutes, or until all the liquid has been absorbed. Sprinkle top with flaked almonds.

Bake for 30 minutes, or until light golden and set. Cool in the tin on a wire rack before turning out.

Serve warm.

SERVES 10

Chocolate brownies

170 g dark cooking chocolate, chopped

60 g unsweetened dark chocolate, chopped

175 g unsalted butter

¾ cup white sugar

2 teaspoons vanilla extract

4 eggs

1 cup plain flour

1 teaspoon salt

1 cup dark chocolate chips

¼ cup chopped walnuts (optional)

Preheat oven to 180°C. Grease and flour a 33-cm × 23-cm baking tin.

Melt cooking chocolate, unsweetened chocolate and butter in a double boiler or in the microwave (see page x). Stir until smooth and set aside to cool.

Once the chocolate is lukewarm, stir in sugar and vanilla. Add eggs one at a time, stirring well after each addition. Stir in sifted flour and salt until just combined, then stir in chocolate chips.

Pour mixture into prepared tin and smooth the top. Sprinkle over chopped walnuts. Bake for 25–30 minutes, or until a skewer inserted comes out clean. Cool in the tin on a wire rack.

Cut into squares and serve at room temperature.

MAKES 24

Chocolate fondue

1 × 250-g block milk or dark chocolate

½ cup cream

fresh fruit, chopped into chunks
   – e.g. strawberries, pear, apple,
   banana, cherries

Melt the chocolate with the cream in a fondue, a double boiler, or in the microwave (see page x).

Serve from the fondue or transfer the melted chocolate to a serving bowl.

Give each person a small fork for dipping fruit into the melted chocolate.

SERVES 6–8

Chocolate ganache tarts

2 sheets shortcrust pastry

200 g dark chocolate, chopped

200 g milk chocolate, chopped

¾ cup thickened cream

1 tablespoon Amaretto

8 macaroons, crumbled

Preheat oven to 200°C. Lightly grease eight 7-cm flan tins.

Line each tin with pastry, trimming off any excess. Bake for 10 minutes, until golden. Remove pastry from tins and set aside to cool on a wire rack.

Heat chocolate and cream in a double boiler or in the microwave (see page x), stirring until chocolate has melted. Stir in Amaretto.

Spoon chocolate mixture into cooled pastry cases and sprinkle with macaroons. Refrigerate for 30 minutes before serving.

SERVES 8

Chocolate hazelnut mousse

225 g dark cooking chocolate, chopped

3 tablespoons water

3 egg yolks

¼ cup icing sugar

½ cup ground roasted hazelnuts

2 tablespoons Frangelico

1½ cups thickened cream

chopped roasted hazelnuts, to serve

Melt chocolate (see page x). Stir until smooth and set aside to cool a little.

In the top of a double boiler (or in a metal bowl set over a saucepan of simmering water), mix together water, egg yolks and sifted icing sugar. Whisk for about 5 minutes, until frothy. Remove from heat and beat for about 3 minutes, until thick. Fold in chocolate, then ground hazelnuts and Frangelico.

In a separate bowl, beat cream until stiff peaks form. Fold a third of the cream into the chocolate mixture. Gradually fold in remaining cream.

Spoon mousse into pretty glasses and chill until cold. Garnish with chopped hazelnuts to serve.

SERVES 10

Chocolate profiteroles

PASTRY

100 g unsalted butter

1 cup water

1 cup plain flour

pinch of salt

4 eggs

CUSTARD

2 tablespoons custard powder

1 tablespoon cocoa

⅓ cup white sugar

1 cup milk

1 egg

1 teaspoon vanilla extract

125 g unsalted butter

SAUCE

150 g dark cooking chocolate, chopped

3 tablespoons crème de cacao (optional)

For pastry, bring butter and water to the boil in a saucepan. Reduce heat, then add sifted flour and salt all at once. Stir over low heat for 1–2 minutes, until smooth and starting to form a ball. Transfer to a bowl and add eggs one at a time, beating well after each addition. Cover loosely and set aside to cool for about an hour.

Preheat oven to 220°C and grease two baking trays.

Place tablespoonfuls of mixture onto prepared baking trays. Bake for 20–25 minutes, until golden and puffed up.　❯

Remove profiteroles and turn oven off. Quickly make a small incision in each profiterole with a sharp knife. Return to oven and leave to cool for at least 10 minutes with door ajar. Remove and cool completely.

For custard, combine custard powder, cocoa, sugar, milk and egg together in a saucepan. Bring to the boil, then simmer for 2 minutes. Remove from heat and add vanilla. Set aside to cool. Cream butter, then gradually beat in custard mixture.

Use a piping bag with round tip to pipe the custard into the incision in each puff.

For sauce, melt chocolate (see page x). Stir in crème de cacao if using.

Arrange profiteroles in individual bowls (three or four per person), and drizzle over warm chocolate sauce to serve.

SERVES 10–12

Chocolate self-saucing pudding in the microwave

1 cup self-raising flour

⅓ cup cocoa

¾ cup white sugar

1 tablespoon butter, melted

½ cup milk

1 teaspoon vanilla extract

¾ cup soft brown sugar, firmly packed

1¾ cups boiling water

Sift together flour, 2 tablespoons of the cocoa and white sugar. Mix in butter combined with milk and vanilla. Beat until smooth.

Pour mixture into a greased 10-cup microwave-safe dish. Combine brown sugar and remaining cocoa and sprinkle over mixture. Carefully pour boiling water over pudding.

Elevate pudding and cook on HIGH for 8 minutes, rotating the dish occasionally. Remove, cover and let stand for 5 minutes (pudding will continue to cook).

Serve warm with custard, cream or ice-cream.

SERVES 4–6

Chocolate semifreddo

250 g dark cooking chocolate
6 eggs, separated
⅓ cup brandy
1½ cups cream

Line a 1-litre freezer-proof container with plastic film.

Melt chocolate (see page x). Allow to cool a little, then stir in egg yolks one at a time. Mix in brandy.

In a separate bowl, whip cream until soft peaks form. Gently fold cream into chocolate mixture.

In another bowl, whip egg whites until soft peaks form. Gently fold into chocolate mixture. Pour mixture into prepared container and freeze for 4 hours, or until firm.

SERVES 6

Chocolate torte

TORTE

80 g dark cooking chocolate,
   chopped

3 eggs

100 g castor sugar

60 g plain flour

TOPPING

⅔ cup thickened cream

225 g milk chocolate, chopped

100 g mascarpone

Preheat oven to 180°C. Grease a 21-cm springform tin.

For torte, melt chocolate (see page x). Beat eggs and sugar until thick and creamy. Fold in melted chocolate and sifted flour.

Pour into prepared tin and bake for 20 minutes, or until a skewer inserted comes out clean. Cool in the tin on a wire rack.

For topping, heat cream and chocolate over low heat. Stir until chocolate has melted. Set aside to cool a little. Once cooled, stir in mascarpone.

Remove torte from tin and spread topping over using a palette knife. Refrigerate 4 hours (or overnight) until firm.

SERVES 8

Chocolate truffles

125 g butter

1¾ cups icing sugar

⅓ cup cocoa

1 tablespoon rum

1 egg white, lightly beaten

⅓ cup desiccated coconut

½ cup chopped sultanas

½ cup finely chopped walnuts

chocolate sprinkles or dessicated
  coconut, for coating

Cream butter, then beat in sifted icing sugar and cocoa. Add rum and egg
white and beat until combined. Fold in coconut, sultanas and walnuts.

Shape teaspoonfuls into balls, then roll in sprinkles or coconut to coat
(or coat half with sprinkles, and half with coconut).

Serve at room temperature.

MAKES 36

Chocolate zucchini cake

1¼ cups plain flour

pinch of salt

½ teaspoon bicarbonate of soda

¼ cup cocoa

¼ teaspoon ground cinnamon

60 g softened butter

¼ cup vegetable oil

¾ cup castor sugar

1 teaspoon finely grated
   orange zest

1 teaspoon vanilla extract

1 egg

1 cup grated zucchini

¼ cup milk

100 g dark cooking chocolate,
   chopped

Preheat oven to 180°C. Lightly grease a 23-cm ring tin.

Sift together flour, salt, bicarbonate of soda, cocoa and cinnamon.

In a separate bowl, cream butter, oil, sugar, orange zest and vanilla. Add egg and mix until combined, then stir in zucchini. Add flour mixture and milk and beat until combined.

Pour into prepared tin and bake for 30 minutes, or until a skewer inserted comes out clean.

Melt dark chocolate (see page x) and drizzle over cake before serving.

SERVES 8–10

Christmas pudding

250 g softened butter

1 cup white sugar

5 eggs

2 tablespoons treacle

500 g sultanas

1 kg raisins, chopped

100 g mixed peel, chopped

4 cups fresh breadcrumbs

1 cup plain flour

1 teaspoon ground nutmeg

1 teaspoon mixed spice

1 teaspoon ground cinnamon

1 teaspoon bicarbonate of soda

½ cup brandy

Cream butter and sugar, then add eggs one at a time, beating well after each addition. Add treacle and beat until combined.

Stir in sultanas, raisins, mixed peel and breadcrumbs. In a separate bowl, sift together flour, nutmeg, mixed spice, cinnamon and bicarbonate of soda. Fold into fruit mixture. Stir in brandy.

Spoon mixture into scalded and floured pudding cloth and tie up. Boil gently for 6 hours, topping saucepan up with boiling water as necessary.

Store in a cool dry place for at least 3 weeks before serving.

Boil pudding for 2 hours to reheat before serving.

SERVES 12

Christmas pudding ice-cream

50 g chopped toasted almonds

200 g raisins, sultanas, currants and chopped candied peel

⅓ cup rum

1 litre chocolate ice-cream

¼ cup green and red glacé cherries, chopped

1 teaspoon ground cinnamon

1 teaspoon mixed spice

glacé cherries or holly leaves, to serve

Soak almonds and dried fruit in the rum overnight. Chill a 2-litre pudding basin in the freezer.

Soften chocolate ice-cream a little, then mix in fruit mixture, cherries and spices until evenly combined.

Spoon mixture into chilled pudding basin and smooth top. Freeze for at least 5 hours, or overnight.

To serve, unmould onto serving plate and decorate with glacé cherries or holly leaves.

SERVES 6–8

Coconut balls

230 g softened unsalted butter

¼ cup icing sugar

2 cups plain flour

pinch of salt

2 cups desiccated coconut

icing sugar, for coating

Preheat oven to 180°C.

Cream butter and sugar until light and fluffy. Add sifted flour and salt and mix until just combined. Stir in coconut.

Roll mixture into 3-cm balls and place onto a baking tray (leave 5 cm between each ball to allow for spreading).

Bake for 15–20 minutes, until just beginning to brown. Allow to cool a little, then roll in icing sugar to coat.

Cool to room temperature before serving with tea or coffee.

MAKES 32

Coconut lemon risotto

3 cups coconut milk

zest of 1 lemon, cut into strips

40 g butter

1 cup arborio rice

½ cup white sugar

Preheat oven to 190°C. Lightly grease a shallow baking dish.

Place the coconut milk, lemon zest and butter in a saucepan and heat until hot but not boiling. Pour the coconut milk mixture into the baking dish and add the rice and sugar. Stir and cover tightly with a lid or foil.

Bake for 30 minutes or until creamy and only a little moist. Stir and remove the lemon zest.

Serve hot with stewed or fresh fruit.

SERVES 6

Coconut meringue cake

120 g butter

1½ cups castor sugar

3 eggs, separated

1 teaspoon vanilla extract

1¼ cups self-raising flour

½ cup milk

1 cup desiccated coconut

Preheat oven to 180°C. Grease and line a 22-cm springform tin.

Cream butter and ½ a cup of the sugar, then beat in egg yolks and vanilla. Add sifted flour and milk and beat until combined. Pour mixture into prepared tin.

In a clean bowl, whip egg whites until stiff peaks form. Add remaining sugar and beat until glossy. Gently fold in coconut.

Pour meringue mixture over cake mixture in tin and smooth top. Bake for 45 minutes, until risen and crisp on top.

SERVES 8

Coeurs à la crème
with raspberry sauce

COEURS À LA CRÈME

250 g ricotta or cream cheese

½ cup icing sugar

1 teaspoon vanilla extract

1 teaspoon finely grated
lemon zest

1 cup sour cream or whipped
thickened cream

SAUCE

350 g raspberries, fresh
or frozen (defrosted)

1 tablespoon castor sugar

1 teaspoon freshly squeezed
lemon juice

NOTE: This recipe requires coeurs à la crème moulds, which have holes in the base to allow liquid to drain out.

If using ricotta cheese, drain in muslin or cheesecloth overnight to remove excess moisture.

Line six coeurs à la crème moulds with lightly dampened muslin or cheesecloth.

Beat ricotta (or cream cheese), with sifted icing sugar, vanilla and lemon zest until smooth. Fold in sour cream (or whipped cream).

Pour mixture into lined moulds. Place on a baking tray to catch drips, cover and refrigerate 6 hours or overnight.

For the sauce, blend all ingredients in a food processor until smooth. Strain through a plastic sieve to remove seeds if desired and refrigerate until needed.

Turn hearts out onto individual serving plates and carefully peel off cloth. Serve drizzled with raspberry sauce.

SERVES 6

Coffee cheesecake

1 × 250 g packet chocolate ripple
   biscuits, finely crushed

80 g unsalted butter, melted

½ cup cream

1 tablespoon instant coffee
   granules

2 teaspoons vanilla extract

900 g cream cheese, at room
   temperature

1¼ cups white sugar

4 eggs

2 tablespoons plain flour

1 cup dark chocolate chips

Preheat oven to 180°C and grease a 23-cm springform tin.

For base, mix together crushed biscuits and butter. Press mixture firmly
into base of prepared tin. Wrap outside of the tin in three layers of foil.
Bake for 10–15 minutes, until firm. Cool.

For filling, combine cream, instant coffee and vanilla in a small bowl.
Set aside.

In a separate bowl, beat cream cheese and sugar until smooth. Add
eggs, one at a time, beating after each addition until just blended. Beat
in sifted flour.

Stir cream mixture until coffee granules dissolve, then beat into cream cheese mixture. Stir in chocolate chips.

Pour filling into tin. Bake in a bain-marie (see page ix) for 50–60 minutes, until edges have puffed up and centre is just set. Cool in the tin on a wire rack for 30 minutes, then chill in the refrigerator overnight.

Before serving, decorate with grated chocolate or sifted icing sugar mixed with powdered drinking chocolate.

SERVES 14–16

Coffee meringues
with caramel sauce

1 cup castor sugar

2 tablespoons instant coffee
  granules

5 egg whites

pinch of salt

½ cup water

1 tablespoon instant coffee
  granules

½ cup castor sugar

Preheat oven to 250°C. Lightly grease eight ramekins.

For meringue, mix together sugar and instant coffee.

Using an electric mixer on medium speed, beat egg whites with salt until
they just form soft peaks. Continue beating while adding sugar mixture
a little at a time. Turn speed to high and beat until stiff peaks form.

Spoon meringue mixture into prepared ramekins, making each into
a swirled peak.

Place ramekins on a baking tray and bake for only 4–5 minutes, until
meringues are slightly puffed and coloured (they will still be very soft).

Cool in ramekins on a wire rack for 30 minutes, then transfer to the
refrigerator and chill at least 3 hours before serving.

For sauce, dissolve coffee granules in half the water.

Put sugar and remaining water into a heavy-based saucepan and bring to the boil, stirring until sugar has dissolved. Boil for about 10 minutes, without stirring, until mixture turns a rich golden colour. (Swirl pan occasionally.) Remove from heat and carefully pour in coffee mixture. Stir until well combined. Transfer syrup to a metal bowl and set aside to cool for about 20 minutes.

To serve, drizzle each meringue with a tablespoon of sauce and top with a dollop of whipped cream.

SERVES 8

Crème brulée

5 egg yolks

2 tablespoons castor sugar

1 teaspoon vanilla extract

2 cups thickened cream

soft brown sugar, to dust

Preheat oven to 160°C and grease six half-cup ramekins.

Beat together egg yolks, sugar and vanilla until thick and creamy. Heat cream and gradually whisk into egg mixture. Pour into a double boiler (or a metal bowl set over a saucepan of simmering water) and continue whisking until thick enough to coat the back of a metal spoon.

Pour custard into ramekins. Bake in a bain-marie (see page ix) for 20 minutes or until just set. Chill for 1 hour.

Dust tops with brown sugar. Put under a very hot grill for a few seconds (or use a mini blowtorch) to caramelise the sugar.

Serve with fresh fruit of the season.

SERVES 6

Crème caramel

CARAMEL

1¼ cups castor sugar

⅔ cup water

CUSTARD

5 eggs

3 egg yolks

½ cup castor sugar

1 teaspoon vanilla extract

1 cup milk

2 cups cream

Preheat oven to 150°C and grease eight ½-cup ramekins.

For caramel, stir sugar and water over low heat until sugar dissolves. Bring to the boil and boil without stirring until syrup turns a light golden brown. (Swirl pan occasionally.) Remove from heat and cool a little. Carefully pour caramel into the ramekins. Swirl so that the mixture coats the sides of each ramekin.

For custard, cream eggs, yolks, sugar and vanilla. Heat milk and cream until almost simmering, then slowly whisk into creamed mixture. Beat gently until sugar dissolves. Strain mixture through a sieve, then pour into the ramekins. Bake in a bain-marie (see page ix) for 30–35 minutes or until set. Refrigerate at least 8 hours before serving.

Carefully turn out onto individual plates to serve.

SERVES 8

Crêpes suzette

CRÊPES

1½ cups plain flour

pinch of salt

3 eggs

450 ml milk

2 tablespoons butter, melted

1 tablespoon cognac

oil, for frying

SAUCE

50 g unsalted butter

⅓ cup icing sugar

⅔ cup orange juice

1 tablespoon finely grated
orange zest

1 teaspoon finely grated
lemon zest

2 tablespoons Cointreau

Blend sifted flour and salt in a food processor. With the processor running, add eggs and a third of the milk. Once blended, add remaining milk, melted butter and cognac and process until smooth. Pour into a jug and refrigerate for at least an hour before using.

Brush a crêpe pan or heavy frying pan with oil and set over medium heat. Once pan is hot, pour in a thin layer of mixture, tipping out any excess. Cook for 1 minute, until golden, then turn and cook the other side for about 30 seconds. (Consider the first crêpe a test run, and subsequently adjust the amount of batter you use and the temperature of the pan according to the result.)

Stack crêpes on a plate and keep warm while you finish cooking the rest of the batter. Brush the pan with oil between each crêpe.

For the sauce, melt butter in cleaned frying pan, then add remaining ingredients and warm for 3–4 minutes. One at a time, fold each crêpe into four to make a triangle shape and heat in the sauce for a few minutes.

Serve immediately, drizzled with any left-over sauce.

SERVES 6

Danish almond cake

dry breadcrumbs, for coating

200 g almonds

200 g castor sugar

4 egg whites

150 g dark cooking chocolate, chopped

vanilla ice-cream and fresh
    strawberries, to serve

Preheat oven to 180°C. Grease a 23-cm ring tin with butter and coat thoroughly with breadcrumbs.

Chop almonds finely, or grind in a food processor. Combine almonds and sugar in a large bowl.

Whip egg whites until stiff peaks form. Gently fold almond mixture into egg whites a third at a time, until just combined.

Pour mixture into prepared tin and bake for 30–45 minutes, or until golden and firm to touch (cover loosely with foil if browning too quickly). Remove from the oven and cool in the tin on a wire rack before turning out. Cake will sink on cooling.

Once cake has cooled, melt chocolate (see page x) and spread over entire cake using a plastic spatula. Chill until chocolate has set, then transfer to a serving plate.

To serve, fill the hole in the centre of the cake with large scoops of ice-cream and decorate with strawberries.

SERVES 8–10

Date and pecan tart

PASTRY

1½ cups plain flour

1 tablespoon icing sugar

pinch of salt

130 g cold unsalted butter,
   cut into small pieces

1 egg yolk

1–2 tablespoons cold water

FILLING

375 g dates, chopped

¼ cup brandy

120 g butter

⅔ cup soft brown sugar

¾ cup pecans

½ cup cream

1 egg

Preheat oven to 190°C and grease 20-cm loose-bottomed flan tin.

For pastry, sift together flour, icing sugar and salt. Rub butter into flour mixture until it resembles breadcrumbs. Combine egg yolk and water and add enough to the flour mixture to form a stiff dough. Knead a little on a lightly floured surface. Roll pastry out into a round piece 26 cm across, and use to line the tin.

For filling, combine dates, brandy, butter and sugar in a saucepan. Simmer about 10 minutes, until dates are soft. Set aside to cool a little. Once mixture is lukewarm, stir in pecans, cream and egg. Spoon filling into pastry shell. Bake for 15 minutes, then reduce oven temperature to 170°C and cook a further 30 minutes.

SERVES 8

Dates with chocolate sauce

SAUCE

150 ml cream

¼ cup milk

150 g dark cooking chocolate, chopped

30 g butter

30 dates, pitted

1 cup toasted flaked almonds

For sauce, heat cream and milk until boiling. Remove from heat and add the chocolate. Set aside for 5 minutes to let chocolate soften, then stir until smooth. Stir in butter until melted and sauce is shiny.

Divide dates into individual serving bowls and drizzle with warm chocolate sauce. Sprinkle over almonds.

Serve immediately with cream or ice-cream.

SERVES 6

Devil's food cake

CAKE

2¼ cups plain flour

3 teaspoons baking powder

½ teaspoon salt

⅔ cup cocoa

1¼ cups castor sugar

3 eggs

150 g butter

1 cup water

FILLING

1 cup thickened cream

1 tablespoon icing sugar

1 tablespoon Tia Maria
(or other liqueur)

200 g strawberries, hulled
and quartered

ICING

1½ cups cream

400 g dark cooking chocolate,
chopped

Preheat oven to 180°C. Grease and line a 23-cm round cake tin.

For cake, sift flour, baking powder, salt and cocoa into a bowl. Mix
well. Add sugar, eggs, butter and water and beat for several minutes
until well combined.

Pour mixture into prepared tin and bake for 50–60 minutes, or until
a skewer inserted comes out clean. Cool in the tin for 15 minutes,
then turn out and cool completely on a wire rack.

For filling, whip cream, icing sugar and liqueur until soft peaks form. Fold in strawberries. Refrigerate until needed.

Using a long bread knife, cut cake in half horizontally. Place one half on a serving plate and spread with the cream filling. Top with the other cake half.

For icing, bring cream to the boil and pour over chocolate. Leave for 1 minute to soften. Carefully stir the ganache until smooth. Set aside to cool a little.

Using a palette knife, spread the icing over the top of the cake. Decorate with grated chocolate and whole strawberries if desired.

SERVES 10

Easy fruit pudding with brandy sauce

2 cups plain flour

1 cup white sugar

1 cup currants

1 cup dates

1 cup dried figs

1 tablespoon butter

1¾ cups boiling water

3 teaspoons bicarbonate of soda

juice and zest of ½ a lemon

SAUCE

250 g softened butter

⅓ cup icing sugar

¼ cup brandy

½ teaspoon ground nutmeg

For pudding, sift flour into a large bowl and mix in sugar and dried fruits. Dissolve butter in half the boiling water and add to the fruit mixture. Dissolve the bicarbonate of soda in the remaining water and add to the fruit mixture. Add the lemon juice and zest. Mix until all ingredients are well combined.

Transfer mixture to a greased 2-cup pudding steamer and steam for 2½ hours.

For sauce, cream the butter and sugar until light and fluffy. Gradually add the brandy, mixing until well combined. Stir in nutmeg.

Serve pudding hot with brandy sauce on the side.

SERVES 6

Eton mess

300 g strawberries, hulled and quartered

2 tablespoons sweet sherry

2 teaspoons castor sugar

1½ cups thickened cream

6 large bought meringues (or 1 bought pavlova),
    broken into pieces

Soak strawberries in sherry and sugar for 30 minutes.

Whip cream until it forms soft peaks. Drain strawberries
and beat reserved liquid into cream.

Gently fold strawberries and meringue into cream.

Serve in individual bowls or glasses.

SERVES 4−6

Flourless chocolate roll with coffee cream

CAKE

170 g dark cooking chocolate, chopped

¼ cup water

6 large eggs, separated

pinch of salt

⅔ cup castor sugar

icing sugar, to dust

FILLING

2 tablespoons Kahlua

¼ cup icing sugar

1 tablespoon instant coffee granules

1 cup thickened cream

Preheat oven to 180°C. Grease 38-cm by 25-cm shallow baking tin and line with a piece of baking paper slightly bigger than the tray.

For the cake, melt chocolate with water over very low heat, while stirring constantly. Set aside to cool.

Beat egg yolks, salt and half the sugar until thick and pale. Gently fold in cooled melted chocolate.

In a separate bowl, beat egg whites until soft peaks form. Gradually add remaining sugar and beat until stiff peaks form. Fold a third of the egg white mixture into the chocolate mixture until incorporated, then fold in remaining egg whites.

Pour mixture into the prepared baking tin and spread evenly. Bake for 15–20 minutes, until risen and dry to the touch. Place tin on a wire rack and cover cake with a damp tea towel. Let stand 5 minutes, then remove tea towel and leave to cool to room temperature. Dust with icing sugar.

Cover cake with a large piece of baking paper. Place a flat baking tray over the paper and carefully invert cake onto it. Very gently peel away the baking paper from the base of the cake.

For the filling, add Kahlua, icing sugar and instant coffee to the cream and stir until coffee has dissolved. Beat until stiff peaks form.

Spread filling onto cake in an even layer. Starting on a long side, use the baking paper to roll the cake into a log. Carefully transfer to a serving platter, seam-side down, before removing the baking paper. Don't worry if the cake cracks a little.

Dust with more icing sugar and cut into slices to serve.

SERVES 12

Flourless orange cake

3 oranges

6 eggs

1 teaspoon vanilla extract

¾ cup raw sugar

400 g almond meal

1½ teaspoons ground cinnamon

2 teaspoons baking powder

Boil the oranges, covered, for 2 hours (adding extra boiling water as necessary).

Preheat oven to 180°C. Lightly grease a 24-cm cake tin (or use 6–8 ×12-cm tins).

Drain and cool oranges, then chop into pieces and remove any pips. Purée oranges (with skin on) in a food processor until smooth.

In a bowl, cream the eggs, vanilla and sugar until thick. Fold in the orange purée, almond meal, cinnamon and baking powder until well combined.

Pour mixture into prepared tin and bake for 1 hour (30 minutes for small cakes), or until a skewer inserted comes out clean.

Cool in the tin on a wire rack for an hour before turning out.

Serve warm or cold with cream, natural yoghurt or sour cream.

SERVES 16

Frangelico bread puddings

⅓ cup sultanas

⅓ cup Frangelico

2 eggs

⅓ cup honey

1 cup milk

1 cup cream

8 slices thickly sliced white
bread, crusts removed

Soak sultanas in the Frangelico for at least 2 hours (or overnight).

Preheat oven to 180°C. Grease four 1-cup ramekins.

Drain sultanas and reserve liquid. Sprinkle half the sultanas evenly into
the ramekins. Combine eggs, honey, milk, cream and reserved Frangelico
in a bowl.

Line each ramekin with a slice of bread, trimming any overhanging edges.
Sprinkle remaining sultanas on top, then cover with another slice of bread.
Divide the egg mixture evenly between the ramekins.

Bake in a bain-marie (see page ix) for 25 minutes, or until set. Remove
from oven and set aside to cool for 5–10 minutes. Serve in the ramekins,
or turned out bottom-side up, with whipped cream. (Add a splash of
Frangelico to the cream before whipping if desired.)

SERVES 4

French blackberry salad

800 g fresh blackberries

juice of 2 limes

¼ cup icing sugar

1 pomegranate

6 figs

Arrange blackberries in individual bowls and sprinkle over lime juice and sugar.

Cut the pomegranate in half and scoop out all the red seeds and pulp, making sure to remove all the bitter yellow membrane. Scatter the seeds and pulp over the blackberries.

Cut a cross into the base of each fig, and open to make a flower shape. Place a fig in the centre of each bowl.

Serve chilled.

SERVES 6

French spice cake

1½ cups water

1 teaspoon anise seeds

1 cup honey

1¼ cups castor sugar

1 teaspoon bicarbonate of soda

6 cups plain flour

1 teaspoon ground cinnamon

1 teaspoon ground nutmeg

pinch of salt

¼ cup candied orange peel, chopped

Preheat oven to 180°C. Grease a large loaf tin.

Bring water to the boil in a small saucepan and add anise seeds. Add honey and sugar and stir until dissolved. Remove from heat and add bicarbonate of soda.

In a bowl, sift together the flour, cinnamon, nutmeg and salt. Stir in candied peel. Strain the honey mixture (discarding the seeds) and gradually add to the flour mixture, stirring constantly. Beat until well combined.

Pour mixture into prepared tin and bake for 1 hour or until a skewer inserted comes out clean.

Serve buttered, with tea or coffee.

SERVES 10

Fresh fruit salad

300 g apricots, stoned and chopped

300 g peaches or nectarines, stoned and chopped

500 g strawberries or blackberries

juice of 1 lime

handful fresh mint, chopped

1 teaspoon icing sugar

Mix all ingredients together. Allow to stand for at least
30 minutes before serving.

Serve with whipped cream or natural yoghurt.

SERVES 6

Frozen berry bombe

600 g vanilla ice-cream, softened

6 tablespoons honey

1 cup slivered almonds

400 g mixed berries, fresh or frozen

Beat the ice-cream, honey and almonds until combined. Fold in berries, taking care not to squash them.

Spoon mixture into a freezer-proof container, cover with a lid or plastic film and freeze at least 1 hour, until firm.

SERVES 8

Frozen honey cheesecake

BASE

100 g finely crushed almonds

150 g plain sweet biscuits, finely
crushed

½ cup castor sugar

100 g unsalted butter, melted

FILLING

250 g mascarpone

250 g cream cheese, at room
temperature

1 × 395-ml tin condensed milk

3 tablespoons honey

1¼ cups cream

1 teaspoon ground cinnamon

1 teaspoon cocoa

Preheat oven to 180°C and grease a 23-cm springform tin.

For base, mix together all ingredients and press firmly into base
of prepared tin. Bake for 10–15 minutes, until firm. Cool.

For the filling, beat mascarpone and cream cheese until smooth.
Add condensed milk and honey and beat until combined. Whip cream
until soft peaks form, then gently fold in. Pour mixture into prepared tin.
Sift cinnamon and cocoa over the top and gently swirl through a fork
or skewer to create a pattern.

Cover and freeze for at least 4 hours, until frozen.

SERVES 8–10

Frozen orange mousse cake

BASE

1 × 250-g packet ginger-nut
  biscuits, finely crushed

¼ cup castor sugar

100 g unsalted butter, melted

MOUSSE

1 cup castor sugar

½ cup freshly squeezed orange
  juice

6 egg yolks

2 tablespoons Grand Marnier

2 cups thickened cream

1 tablespoon finely grated
  orange zest

1 teaspoon finely grated
  lemon zest

sugared orange slices,
  to serve (optional)

Preheat oven to 170°C. Lightly grease a 23-cm springform tin.

For base, mix together crushed biscuits, sugar and butter. Press mixture firmly into base of prepared tin. Bake for 10–15 minutes, until firm. Cool.

For mousse, whisk together sugar, orange juice and egg yolks in a double boiler (or use a metal bowl set over a saucepan of simmering water). Whisk for 4 minutes, then transfer to a bowl. Beat for 5 minutes, until thick and cool, then mix in Grand Marnier.

In a separate bowl, whisk cream and grated orange and lemon zests until stiff peaks form. Gently fold in egg mixture. Pour mousse onto base. Cover and freeze for 6 hours (or overnight).   >

Unmould onto a serving platter. If desired, garnish with sugared orange slices. Serve immediately (this dessert will begin to melt once removed from the freezer), with whipped cream.

SERVES 10–12

Fruit and chocolate bread pudding

1 stale Vienna loaf, sliced

3 tablespoons butter, cut into small pieces

⅓ cup white sugar

½ cup powdered drinking chocolate

3 tablespoons almond essence

750 g mixed dried fruit

Preheat oven to 180°C and grease a 22-cm square baking dish.

Soak bread slices in water until moist, then squeeze out excess water. Combine bread with remaining ingredients and mix thoroughly. Bake for 1 hour. Serve warm with cream.

SERVES 12

Fruit fritters

1 cup self-raising flour

⅔ cup skim milk

1 tablespoon olive oil

2 egg whites

pinch of salt

1 teaspoon castor sugar

2 bananas, peeled and sliced
    lengthways

6 pineapple rings

2 apples, peeled, cored
    and thickly sliced

2 oranges, peeled, thickly sliced
    and seeds removed

½ cup castor sugar

sunflower oil for deep-frying

icing sugar, to dust

For batter, mix sifted flour, milk and oil until smooth. In a separate bowl, whisk egg whites until soft peaks form. Add salt and sugar, then whisk until stiff peaks form. Gently fold egg whites into flour mixture.

Sprinkle fruit with sugar. Heat oil until very hot but not smoking. Dip each piece of fruit into the batter and deep-fry for 3–5 minutes, until golden brown. Remove with a slotted spoon or tongs and drain on kitchen paper.

Serve hot, dusted with icing sugar.

SERVES 6

Fruity currant parcels

⅓ cup currants

⅓ cup sultanas

⅓ cup raisins

¼ cup candied peel, chopped

¼ cup soft brown sugar

60 g unsalted butter, melted

2 tablespoons freshly squeezed
    lemon juice

1½ teaspoons finely grated
    lemon zest

½ teaspoon ground nutmeg

½ teaspoon ground cinnamon

1 sheet frozen puff pastry,
    thawed

1 egg, lightly beaten

2 teaspoons castor sugar

Preheat oven to 190°C. Grease a baking tray.

For filling, combine fruit, sugar, butter, lemon juice and zest, and spices in a bowl.

Lightly flour a work surface and roll pastry out to half a centimetre in thickness. Cut pastry into four squares, each measuring about 14-cm across. Place a quarter of the filling onto one triangular half of each square, leaving a 1-cm border around the edge. Brush the edges of each square with egg. Fold the pastry over the filling to create a triangle. Press the edges down firmly to seal.

Brush each parcel with beaten egg and sprinkle with sugar. Bake for 20 minutes, or until golden brown. Cool on the tray for 5 minutes, before transferring to a wire rack to cool further.

Serve warm with cream or ice-cream.

SERVES 4

Golden bread and butter pudding

4 slices white bread

3 tablespoons golden syrup

3 eggs, beaten

1½ cups cream

1 cup milk

1 teaspoon vanilla extract

3 tablespoons castor sugar

½ cup chopped dried apricots

ground cinnamon or nutmeg,
   for sprinkling

Preheat the oven to 160°C and grease a pie dish.

Spread the bread slices with golden syrup and cut each into four triangles.
Arrange in an overlapping pattern in the pie dish.

Whisk together the eggs, cream, milk, vanilla and castor sugar. Pour
mixture over the bread, then sprinkle with the chopped apricots and
cinnamon or nutmeg.

Bake for 25 minutes or until the custard has set.

Serve hot, with ice-cream.

SERVES 4

Grand Marnier berry trifle

6 thin sponge fingers

⅓ cup Grand Marnier

2 eggs, separated

⅓ cup castor sugar

2 tablespoons finely grated
orange zest

1 tablespoon finely grated
lemon zest

1 cup thickened cream

250 g mixed berries, fresh
or frozen (defrosted)

¼ cup icing sugar

Break the sponge fingers into pieces and put them into a 6-cup glass bowl, trifle dish or six individual glasses. Using a tablespoon, sprinkle over half the Grand Marnier. Set aside.

Beat the egg yolks and sugar until thick, then beat in orange and lemon zest.

In a separate bowl, beat the egg whites until stiff peaks form. Fold egg whites into egg yolk mixture. Beat cream until soft peaks form, then fold into egg mixture. Cover and refrigerate for 1 hour.

Gently toss berries with icing sugar and remaining Grand Marnier. Let stand for 1 hour.

To serve, spoon cream over the soaked sponge fingers, and top with berries.

SERVES 6

Green tea ice-cream

4 tablespoons green tea leaves

200 ml water

3 egg yolks

300 ml milk

2 tablespoons castor sugar

300 ml cream

NOTE: This recipe requires an ice-cream maker.

Place tea leaves and water in a saucepan and slowly bring to the boil. Remove from heat and set aside for 5 minutes. Strain and discard tea leaves.

Lightly whisk egg yolks in a clean saucepan. Add milk and sugar and mix well. Stir constantly over low heat until mixture has thickened. Remove from the heat and set saucepan in a dish of ice water to help it cool.

Add green tea liquid to the egg mixture and mix well. Add cream and mix until well combined.

Pour the mixture into an ice-cream maker and freeze according to the machine's instructions.

SERVES 6

Hazelnut bavarian

2 tablespoons water

1 tablespoon gelatine

¾ cup milk

½ cup castor sugar

6 egg yolks

160 g finely ground roasted hazelnuts

1 teaspoon vanilla extract

1½ cups thickened cream

cocoa and icing sugar, to serve

Grease six ⅔-cup dariole moulds.

Pour water into a small bowl and sprinkle over gelatine. Let stand 1 minute. Set bowl in a tray of boiling water and stir until gelatine has dissolved. In a saucepan heat milk to almost boiling.

In a double boiler (or a metal bowl set over a saucepan of simmering water), whisk sugar and egg yolks until pale, then gradually whisk in hot milk. Stir until mixture thickens, then remove from the heat and stir in gelatine, hazelnuts and vanilla. Set aside for 15 minutes, then refrigerate until almost starting to set.

Whip cream until soft peaks form. Gently fold into hazelnut mixture. Spoon into prepared moulds and refrigerate 6 hours (or overnight).

To serve, unmould onto individual serving plates and dust with cocoa mixed with icing sugar.

SERVES 6

Hazelnut chocolate tart

½ cup roasted hazelnuts,
  skins removed

1 cup plain flour

1 tablespoon castor sugar

pinch of salt

60 g cold unsalted butter,
  cut into small pieces

1 egg

200 g dark cooking chocolate,
  chopped

½ cup milk

¼ cup castor sugar

¼ teaspoon salt

2 egg yolks

1 tablespoon Frangelico

1 cup crème fraîche

Preheat oven to 180°C and grease a 24-cm loose-bottomed flan tin.

For pastry, blend hazelnuts with flour, sugar and salt in a food processor until finely ground. Add butter and process until mixture resembles fine breadcrumbs (don't worry if there are still some small lumps of butter). Add egg and process until mixture begins to clump together.

Press mixture into the flan tin, covering the base and sides. Chill for 10 minutes. Bake blind (see page x) for about 15 minutes, until the top edges are golden. Remove baking paper and weights and return shell to oven. Bake a further 10 minutes, until bottom and sides are golden.

Cool in the tin on a wire rack for 10 minutes. Reduce oven temperature to 160°C.

For filling, put chocolate into a bowl. Bring milk, sugar and salt to the boil, stirring constantly. Pour over the chocolate and let stand until chocolate has melted. Stir until smooth and slightly cooled, then mix in egg yolks and Frangelico. Mix in crème fraîche.

Pour mixture into pastry shell. Bake for 20–25 minutes, until set. Cool completely in the tin on a wire rack. Chill in the refrigerator for at least an hour, until firm.

Serve at room temperature, with cream.

SERVES 10

Hazelnut meringue torte with cappuccino cream

MERINGUE

1 cup roasted hazelnuts, skins removed

6 egg whites

1 cup castor sugar

⅓ cup plain flour

FILLING

1 tablespoon instant coffee granules

2 tablespoons Kahlua or Frangelico

1½ cups thickened cream

¼ cup icing sugar

TOPPING

¼ cup roasted hazelnuts, skins removed

100 g dark chocolate, grated

Preheat oven to 180°C. Lightly grease and flour two 20-cm round cake tins.

For meringue, grind hazelnuts in a food processor until finely ground. Beat egg whites until soft peaks form. Gradually add sugar and beat until stiff, glossy peaks form. Gently fold in ground hazelnuts and then sifted flour until well combined.

Divide mixture evenly between prepared tins and smooth the tops. Bake for 30–35 minutes, until firm and light golden. Turn out onto wire racks to cool. ➤

For the filling, dissolve coffee granules in the liqueur. Add to the cream with the sifted icing sugar and beat until soft peaks form.

Place one meringue layer on a serving plate. Spread over half the filling, then place the second meringue layer on top. Spread over remaining filling.

For topping, place hazelnuts in a plastic bag and crush with a rolling pin. Sprinkle the torte with crushed hazelnuts and grated dark chocolate.

SERVES 8

Honey-baked quinces

6 quinces, peeled, halved and cored

3 tablespoons honey

30 g unsalted butter

½ cup sweet dessert wine

Preheat oven to 150°C and grease a baking dish.

Arrange quinces flat-side up in a single layer in the baking dish. Drizzle honey over fruit and dot with butter. Pour over wine. Cover with foil and bake for 2 hours. Turn quinces, re-cover, and bake another 2 hours.

Serve hot with cream or ice-cream.

SERVES 6

Indian rice pudding

⅓ cup basmati rice

2 cups cold water

1½ tablespoons ghee

2 tablespoons raisins

2 tablespoons chopped toasted
  cashews

1 tablespoon chopped toasted
  almonds

5½ cups milk

8 saffron threads

⅓ cup white sugar

pinch of ground cardamom

Rinse rice in cold running water. Add drained rice to 2 cups of cold water and let stand for 1 hour. Drain.

Heat ghee in a small frying pan until hot but not smoking. Add raisins and nuts and cook for about 2 minutes, until golden. Set aside.

Heat milk in a heavy saucepan until it simmers. In a small bowl, soak the saffron in a couple of tablespoons of the hot milk.

Add rice to the pan with the remaining hot milk and simmer for about 10 minutes, stirring frequently, until the rice is cooked. Add sugar and simmer for a further 30 minutes, stirring frequently, until the mixture has thickened. Stir in raisins and nuts, saffron mixture and cardamom and cook for a few minutes more.

Allow to cool a little before serving. If the pudding is too thick, add a little milk or cream.

SERVES 4

Jaffa mousse

175 g dark cooking chocolate, chopped

5 egg yolks

⅓ cup castor sugar

¾ cup cream

½ cup Grand Marnier

2 tablespoons cocoa

2 teaspoons grated orange zest

orange slices, to serve

Melt chocolate (see page x). Set aside to cool a little. In a separate bowl, beat the egg yolks and sugar until pale and thick.

In another bowl, whip cream until soft peaks form. Add Grand Marnier and whip again until soft peaks form.

Mix together warm chocolate and egg mixture. Fold in half the whipped cream, then fold in remaining cream, cocoa and orange zest.

Spoon into individual ramekins, cups or glasses. Refrigerate for at least 2 hours before serving. Garnish with orange slices to serve.

SERVES 4–6

Japanese sesame sweet potato

vegetable oil, for deep-frying

1 kg sweet potatoes, chopped into small chunks

⅓ cup water

½ cup white sugar

2 teaspoons soy sauce

2 tablespoons sesame seeds

Heat the oil in a deep fryer and fry the sweet potatoes at 180°C until golden brown. Drain the sweet potato on kitchen paper.

Heat the water, sugar and soy sauce in a large frying pan over low heat. When the sauce becomes syrupy and sticky, remove from the heat and add the sweet potatoes. Toss to coat each piece with syrup.

Once evenly coated, sprinkle the sweet potato with sesame seeds.

Serve warm.

SERVES 8

Jubilee cake

1½ cups self-raising flour

1 tablespoon castor sugar

pinch of salt

1 cup mixed dried fruit (or any dried fruit)

2 teaspoons grated lemon zest

1 egg

½ cup milk

ICING

2 tablespoons icing sugar

milk, to mix

desiccated coconut, to sprinkle

Preheat oven to 190°C and grease a loaf tin.

Mix sifted flour with castor sugar, salt, dried fruit and lemon zest. Add egg and milk and mix well. Pour mixture into loaf tin and bake for 30 minutes, or until a skewer inserted comes out clean.

To make icing, mix enough milk with the sifted icing sugar to make a thin icing. Pour over the cake while still warm, and sprinkle with coconut.

Allow to cool completely, then slice and spread with butter to serve.

SERVES 6–8

Lavender ice-cream

4–8 stems English lavender, washed

2½ cups cream

½ teaspoon grated lemon zest

½ cup white sugar

4 egg yolks

Chill a metal baking tray in the freezer.

Place lavender, cream and lemon zest in a saucepan and heat until hot but not boiling. Stir in sugar until dissolved. Strain mixture through a fine sieve to remove lavender.

Combine egg yolks and cream mixture in the saucepan and stir over low heat until the consistency of custard (thick enough to coat the back of a metal spoon). Do not boil.

Pour mixture onto chilled tray and leave to cool. Once cool, freeze for 2 hours, or until just frozen around the edges. Scrap into a bowl and beat until slushy. Pour back onto the baking tray and return to the freezer. Repeat this process twice more. Scoop into desired container, cover and freeze until firm.

SERVES 4–6

Lemon and ginger cheesecake

1 × 250-g packet ginger-nut
  biscuits, finely crushed

½ teaspoon ground ginger

¼ cup castor sugar

70 g unsalted butter, melted

1 kg cream cheese, at room
  temperature

1¼ cups castor sugar

4 eggs

1½ cups sour cream

2 tablespoons finely grated
  fresh ginger

2 tablespoons finely grated
  lemon zest

2 tablespoons freshly squeezed
  lemon juice

Preheat oven to 170°C and grease a 23-cm springform tin.

For base, mix together crushed biscuits, ginger, sugar and butter. Press mixture firmly into base of prepared tin. Wrap outside of the tin in three layers of foil. Bake for 10–15 minutes, until firm. Cool.

For filling, beat cream cheese and sugar until smooth. Add eggs, one at a time, beating after each addition until just blended. Then beat in the sour cream, ginger, lemon zest and juice. Pour filling into tin. >

Bake in a bain-marie (see page ix) for about 1 hour and 20 minutes, until edges have puffed up but centre is not completely set. Cool in the tin on a wire rack for 2 hours, then chill in the refrigerator overnight.

Garnish with one of the following (or a combination): lemon slices, lemon leaves, ground ginger, or ginger-nut biscuit crumbs.

SERVES 14–16

Lemon and lime sorbet

1 cup white sugar

2 cups water

1 cup freshly squeezed
   lemon juice

½ cup freshly squeezed
   lime juice

2 egg whites

Chill a metal baking tray in the freezer.

Stir water and sugar over low heat until sugar has dissolved. Bring to the boil, then simmer gently for 5 minutes. Set aside to cool.

Add juices to sugar syrup and stir. Pour into chilled baking tray and freeze for 2 hours. Scrape mixture into a bowl and beat until slushy. Pour back onto the baking tray and return to the freezer. Repeat this process twice more.

Scrape icy mixture into a bowl and beat in egg whites. Scoop into desired container, cover and freeze until firm.

SERVES 4

Lemon delight

30 g softened butter

½ cup castor sugar

½ cup self-raising flour

juice and grated zest of 2 lemons

1 cup milk

2 eggs, separated

Preheat oven to 180°C. Lightly grease a pie dish.

Cream butter and sugar, then add sifted flour and mix until combined. Stir in lemon juice and zest, then add milk and egg yolks.

In a separate bowl, whip egg whites until stiff peaks form. Gently fold into the lemon mixture.

Pour mixture into the pie dish and bake in a bain-marie (see page ix) for 20 minutes, until golden and firm on top.

SERVES 4–6

Lemon soufflés

1 cup milk

60 g butter

¼ cup castor sugar

1 teaspoon finely grated
    lemon zest

¼ cup Limoncello (or other
    lemon liqueur)

2 tablespoons plain flour

1 tablespoon cornflour

4 egg yolks

6 egg whites

Preheat oven to 200°C. Grease six 1-cup soufflé dishes and dust with
castor sugar.

Pour milk into a saucepan and bring to the boil. Remove from heat.

Cream butter, sugar and lemon zest until light and fluffy. Add Limoncello,
sifted flour and cornflour and beat until well combined. Gradually add hot
milk to the mixture while beating constantly. Transfer mixture to a saucepan
and beat over a medium heat until it boils and thickens. Beat in egg yolks
until combined. Pour into a bowl.

In a separate bowl, whisk the egg whites until soft peaks form. Fold a
third of the egg whites into the lemon mixture, then fold in remaining
egg whites. Spoon into dishes, and place onto a baking tray. Bake for
15–20 minutes, until puffed up and golden.

SERVES 6

Lemon tart

1½ cups plain flour

1 tablespoon icing sugar

pinch of salt

130 g cold unsalted butter,
cut into small pieces

1 egg yolk

1–2 tablespoons cold water

5 eggs

¾ cups castor sugar

1–2 tablespoons finely grated
lemon zest

½ cup freshly squeezed
lemon juice

1 cup thickened cream

To make pastry, blend together flour, sugar, and salt in a food processor. Add butter and process until mixture resembles fine breadcrumbs (don't worry if there are still some small lumps of butter). Add egg yolk and water and process until mixture begins to clump together. Roll pastry into a ball, wrap in plastic film and refrigerate for 30 minutes.

On a lightly floured board, roll pastry out into a round piece 30 cm across. Use to line a greased 24-cm loose-bottomed flan tin, covering the base and sides – trim so that pastry is half a centimetre above the rim. Refrigerate another 30 minutes.

Preheat oven to 190°C.

Bake blind (see page x) for about 15 minutes, until the top edges are golden. Remove baking paper and weights and return shell to oven. Bake a further 10–15 minutes, until bottom and sides are golden. Cool in the tin on a wire rack for 10 minutes. Reduce oven temperature to 180°C.

To make filling, whisk together all ingredients until well combined. Pour filling into shell and bake for 20–30 minutes, until filling has almost set – it should still tremble a little when shaken gently. Cool in the tin on a wire rack, then refrigerate until cold.

Dust with icing sugar to serve.

SERVES 8–10

Lime frozen yoghurt

2 litres thick natural (unflavoured) yoghurt

2 teaspoons finely grated lime zest

½ cup freshly squeezed lime juice

⅓ cup golden syrup

½ cup castor sugar

NOTE: This recipe requires an ice-cream maker.

Line a colander with cheesecloth and place over a bowl. Pour yoghurt in, cover and set in the refrigerator to drain for at least 10 hours (or overnight). Discard liquid.

In a food processor, blend half of the drained yogurt with the zest, juice, golden syrup and sugar. Transfer to a bowl and stir in remaining yogurt.

Pour the mixture into an ice-cream maker and freeze according to the machine's instructions.

SERVES 4–6

Lime tartlets

1 cup plain flour

1 tablespoon castor sugar

80 g cold unsalted butter, cut
   into small pieces

1–2 tablespoons cold water

½ cup castor sugar

130 g unsalted butter

4 eggs, lightly beaten

1 tablespoon finely grated
   lime zest

½ cup freshly squeezed
   lime juice

For pastry, sift flour and sugar into a bowl. Rub butter into flour mixture until it resembles breadcrumbs. Add enough water to the mixture to form a stiff dough. Roll into a ball, cover with plastic film and chill for 30 minutes.

Preheat oven to 200°C. Lightly grease twenty 5-cm tart tins.

Roll out the pastry on a lightly floured surface until about 5-mm thick. Use a 6-cm cookie cutter to cut out 20 rounds from the pastry. Use the pastry to line the prepared tins, trimming off any excess.

Bake for 15 minutes, or until light golden. Cool in the tins on a wire rack.

To make the lime filling, combine the sugar, butter, eggs, zest and juice in a saucepan over low heat. Heat gently for 10–15 minutes, stirring occasionally, until mixture thickens. Transfer to a bowl and chill for 3 hours, until thickened and cold.

Spoon lime curd into pastry cases. Dust with icing sugar to serve.

MAKES 20

Loganberry sago

4 tablespoons sago

2 cups water

1 teaspoon butter

1 cup white sugar

2 cups loganberries
   (or blackberries), washed

Stir together sago, water and butter in a saucepan. When the mixture starts to boil, add the sugar. Cook for 10–15 minutes, or until the sago is clear. Add the loganberries and return to the boil. Take off the heat and cool.

Serve with vanilla ice-cream.

SERVES 4

Macaroon chocolate charlotte

115 g dark cooking chocolate,
   chopped

¼ cup milk

2 tablespoons castor sugar

3 large eggs, separated

2 teaspoons finely grated
   orange zest

pinch of salt

¼ cup brandy

¼ cup water

10–12 large macaroons

Lightly grease a 1-litre charlotte mould (or use any 1-litre mould).

Melt the chocolate (see page x). Set aside to cool. Heat the milk and sugar in a saucepan until almost boiling, then pour over the chocolate and stir until well combined.

Allow to cool, then beat in egg yolks until smooth and shiny. Mix in orange zest and leave to cool completely.

In a separate bowl, beat the egg whites and salt until stiff peaks form. Gently fold half the egg whites into the chocolate mixture, then fold in remaining egg whites.

Combine the brandy and water in a small bowl. Dip each macaroon into the brandy mixture, then use the macaroons (placed flat side down) to line the mould, covering the base and sides. Pour half the chocolate mixture into the mould, then cover with a layer of macaroons. Pour over the remaining chocolate and top with remaining macaroons.

Cover with plastic film and place a weighted plate on top. Refrigerate overnight.

To serve, remove weighted plate and unmould the charlotte onto a serving platter.

SERVES 6

Mango puddings

5 or 6 very ripe mangoes, peeled,
    stoned and chopped
1 tablespoon gelatine
1¼ cups water
½ cup castor sugar
¾ cup evaporated milk

Purée the mangoes in a food processor until smooth (reserve 1 mango for garnish). Rub the pulp through a sieve into a bowl and discard any fibers.

Pour ¼ cup of the water into a small bowl and sprinkle over the gelatine. Let stand 1 minute. Heat remaining water and sugar in a saucepan. Stir until sugar has dissolved, then add gelatine mixture and stir until dissolved. Add puréed mango and heat until just simmering. Remove from heat and stir in evaporated milk. Cool for about 30 minutes, stirring occasionally.

Pour into eight small bowls or glasses and chill, covered, for at least 8 hours (or overnight) before serving. Garnish with thin slices of mango.

SERVES 8

Maple syrup pudding

SYRUP

1¼ cups real maple syrup

¾ cup thickened cream

2 teaspoons cider vinegar

pinch of salt

PUDDING

85 g softened unsalted butter

⅓ cup castor sugar

1 egg

½ teaspoon vanilla extract

1 cup plain flour

1 teaspoon baking powder

¼ teaspoon salt

Preheat oven to 180°C and grease a 20-cm baking dish.

For syrup, put maple syrup, cream, vinegar and salt into a small saucepan and bring to the boil. Set aside.

For pudding, cream butter and sugar until light and fluffy. Beat in egg and vanilla until just combined. In a separate bowl, sift together flour, baking powder and salt. Stir into creamed mixture until just combined.

Pour about half a cup of the syrup mixture into the baking dish. Spoon pudding mixture evenly over the syrup. Pour remaining syrup over.

Bake for 25–35 minutes, until golden and firm to the touch. Serve warm, with cream.

SERVES 6

Marna's cinnamon apple cake

FILLING

2 cooking apples, peeled, cored
  and sliced

1 tablespoon castor sugar

1 teaspoon butter

2 cloves

2 tablespoons water

BASE

85 g softened butter

125 g castor sugar

1 egg, well beaten

1 cup self-raising flour

2 tablespoons cornflour

2 tablespoons ground cinnamon

1 teaspoon cocoa

Preheat oven to 190°C and grease a pie dish.

For the filling, stew all ingredients in a saucepan until the apple
is cooked.

For the base, cream the butter and sugar. Beat in the egg. Sift the flours,
cinnamon and cocoa, and mix in to the creamed mixture.

Turn the dough onto a lightly floured board and knead gently. Divide the
mixture in half, and roll out into two round pieces. Cover the base of the
pie dish with one piece of dough. Pour in the apple mixture. Cover with
the remaining piece of dough. Pinch the edges to seal, and prick the top.

Bake for 20 minutes.

SERVES 6−8

Meringue roulade
with strawberry cream

MERINGUE

5 egg whites

1¼ cups castor sugar

1½ teaspoons cornflour

1 teaspoon cider or white
   vinegar

icing sugar, to dust

FILLING

1 cup thickened cream

3 tablespoons strawberry liqueur
   (optional)

2 tablespoons icing sugar

2 cups fresh strawberries, hulled
   and sliced

Preheat oven to 160°C. Grease a 25-cm × 30-cm Swiss roll tin and line with a piece of baking paper slightly bigger than the tray.

For the meringue, beat egg whites until stiff peaks form. Continue beating and gradually add sugar. Beat until thick and glossy. Add sifted cornflour and vinegar and beat in.

Spoon mixture into prepared tin and spread evenly.

Bake for 15–20 minutes until pale cream, risen and crisp. Cool in the tin on a wire rack.

Once cool, dust with icing sugar. Cover cake with a large piece of baking paper. Place a flat baking tray over the paper and carefully invert meringue onto it. Very gently peel away the baking paper from the base of the meringue.

For the filling, beat cream, liqueur and icing sugar until stiff peaks form. Fold through strawberries.

Spread filling evenly over meringue, leaving a 2-cm border around the edges. Starting on a long side, use the baking paper to roll the meringue into a log. Carefully transfer to a serving platter, seam-side down, before removing the baking paper. Dust with more icing sugar.

Serve chilled, cut into slices.

SERVES 10

Microwave blueberry pudding with chocolate sauce

PUDDING

100 g softened butter

100 g castor sugar

100 g self-raising flour

1½ teaspoons baking powder

1½ cups milk

100 g blueberries

SAUCE

¾ cup cream

100 g dark cooking chocolate, chopped

For pudding, cream butter and sugar. Add sifted flour and baking powder, then stir in milk. Carefully fold in the blueberries. Pour into a greased microwave-safe pudding bowl. Cook on HIGH for 3 minutes.

Allow to cool for 5 minutes.

Meanwhile, for sauce, heat cream on MEDIUM until simmering. Remove and add chocolate. Let stand 1 minute. Stir until chocolate has melted and ganache forms a smooth consistency.

Turn out pudding and serve with chocolate sauce.

SERVES 4

Mocha affogato

¼ cup liqueur of choice (e.g. Amaretto,
    Tia Maria, Baileys, Frangelico)

1½ cups hot espresso coffee

1 litre rich chocolate ice-cream

grated dark chocolate, to serve

Add liqueur to coffee. Spoon ice-cream into serving bowls and pour over coffee. Serve immediately, topped with a little grated chocolate.

SERVES 4

Mocha fudge sundaes

½ cup thickened cream

¼ cup espresso coffee

125 g dark cooking chocolate, chopped

125 g milk chocolate, chopped

½ teaspoon vanilla extract

1 teaspoon ground cinnamon

1 litre vanilla ice-cream

1 litre chocolate ice-cream

1 cup slivered almonds, toasted

1 cup mini marshmallows, chopped

whipped cream (optional)

Bring cream and coffee almost to the boil. Remove from heat and stir in chocolate, vanilla and cinnamon. Stir until chocolate is melted and sauce is smooth.

Scoop vanilla and chocolate ice-cream into bowls. Pour over warm fudge sauce, sprinkle with almonds and marshmallows, and top with whipped cream.

SERVES 8–10

Mocha mousse

130 g dark cooking chocolate, chopped

30 g unsalted butter

2 tablespoons espresso coffee

1 cup thickened cream

3 eggs, separated

1 tablespoon icing sugar

Place the chocolate, butter and coffee in the top of a double boiler (or a metal bowl set over a saucepan of hot water). Stir over hot water (not simmering), until smooth. Remove from the heat and set aside to cool a little.

Whip the cream until it forms soft peaks, then refrigerate.

Whip the egg whites until they almost form soft peaks. Add sugar and beat until soft peaks form.

Stir egg yolks into the warm chocolate. Fold a third of the cream into the chocolate mixture. Fold in half the egg whites until just combined, then fold in remaining whites. Fold in remaining whipped cream.

Spoon mousse into eight pretty glasses or serving dishes. Chill for at least 8 hours (or overnight) before serving.

SERVES 8

Moist chocolate puddings

PUDDING

200 g dark cooking chocolate, chopped

200 g butter, chopped

4 eggs plus 4 egg yolks

½ cup soft brown sugar

¼ cup plain flour

SAUCE

200 g dark cooking chocolate, chopped

1 cup cream

2 tablespoons crème de cacao (optional)

Preheat oven to 180°C. Lightly grease eight 1-cup dariole moulds.

For pudding, melt chocolate and butter in a saucepan over low heat. Stir until melted and smooth. Set aside to cool. Beat together eggs, yolks and sugar until light and fluffy. Stir in melted chocolate mixture, then gently fold in sifted flour. Spoon mixture into prepared darioles. Place moulds on a baking tray and bake for 10 minutes or until set. Set moulds on a wire rack to cool.

For chocolate sauce, heat chocolate and cream in a saucepan over low heat. Stir until chocolate has melted and mixture is smooth. Mix in liqueur if using.

To serve, unmould warm puddings onto individual serving plates and drizzle with chocolate sauce.

SERVES 8

Orange and ginger ricotta cake

1 kg fresh ricotta

½ cup honey

¼ cup freshly squeezed
   orange juice

finely grated zest of 3 oranges

½ teaspoon ground ginger

4 eggs, beaten

¼ cup plain flour

125 g glacé ginger, chopped

orange slices and Cointreau,
   to serve

Preheat oven to 170°C. Lightly grease and flour a 20-cm springform tin.

Break up ricotta then beat until smooth (or blend in a food processor).
Add honey, orange juice and zest, ground ginger and eggs and beat until
smooth. Add sifted flour and beat until combined. Fold in glacé ginger.

Pour mixture into prepared tin and bake for 1 hour, until golden on top but
not completely set in the centre. Turn oven off, open the door slightly and
leave cake to cool in the oven.

Once cool, chill in the refrigerator before removing from the tin.

Serve with orange slices that have been soaked in Cointreau for at least
an hour.

SERVES 12

Orange crème caramels

1 cup castor sugar

100 ml water

600 ml freshly squeezed orange juice

6 eggs, beaten

Preheat oven to 180°C and lightly grease eight ramekins.

In a saucepan, slowly heat half the sugar with the water until the sugar dissolves. Increase heat and boil rapidly until the mixture starts to caramelise. The sauce will get quite dark – but be careful not to let it burn.

Carefully pour caramel into the ramekins. Swirl so that the mixture coats the sides of each ramekin.

Beat together orange juice, eggs and remaining sugar. Once smooth, pour into the ramekins. Bake in a bain-marie (see page ix) for 20 minutes, until just set. Remove from bain-marie and cool ramekins on a wire rack.

Once cool, cover and chill for at least 8 hours (or overnight) until ready to serve.

Carefully turn out onto individual small plates to serve.

SERVES 8

Orange pudding

¾ teaspoon baking soda

1½ tablespoons freshly squeezed orange juice

½ cup raisins

1 tablespoon plain flour

60 g softened unsalted butter

¼ cup castor sugar

pinch of salt

2 eggs

½ cup marmalade

1½ cups fresh wholemeal breadcrumbs

Grease a 6-cup pudding mould.

Mix together the baking soda and orange juice. In a separate bowl, mix the raisins and sifted flour.

In another bowl, cream the butter, sugar and salt until light and fluffy. Add eggs one at a time, beating well after each addition. Add all other ingredients and mix on low speed until well blended.

Spoon mixture into the prepared mould. Cover tightly with foil or a lid. Steam for about 2 hours, until the pudding feels dry and firm to the touch. Cool on a wire rack for 5 minutes, then use a knife to loosen the edges and turn out onto a serving plate.

Serve warm with custard or cream.

SERVES 6

Oranges in red wine

¾ cup white sugar

1 cup water

1 cup red wine

1 cinnamon stick

12 cloves

2 slices of lemon

8 oranges

Dissolve sugar in the water over a medium heat. Add red wine, cinnamon, cloves and lemon slices. Bring to the boil and simmer until syrupy.

Peel oranges and remove pith. Cut into slices and place into a serving dish. Pour the wine syrup over and chill overnight.

Serve with cream or ice-cream.

SERVES 8

Pan-fried bananas
with butterscotch sauce

⅓ cup golden syrup

½ cup soft brown sugar

½ cup castor sugar

¼ cup water

60 g butter

⅔ cup thickened cream

1 teaspoon vanilla extract

BANANAS

4 bananas

1 tablespoon butter

1 tablespoon vegetable oil

For sauce, heat golden syrup, sugars and water in a small saucepan.
Stir over low heat until sugar has dissolved, then increase heat and simmer
without stirring for about 3 minutes, until sauce turns a golden colour.
Remove from heat and add butter. Gently swirl the pan until butter has
dissolved, then stir in cream and vanilla. Cool to room temperature (sauce
will thicken).

Peel bananas and slice each in half lengthways. Heat butter and oil in
a large frying pan over high heat until foaming. Fry bananas for a couple
of minutes on each side, until golden.

Serve bananas immediately, with butterscotch sauce and ice-cream.

SERVES 4

Panna cotta

2 tablespoons water
1¼ teaspoons gelatine
2½ cups cream
½ cup milk
⅓ cup castor sugar
1 teaspoon vanilla extract

Pour water into a small bowl and sprinkle over the gelatine. Let stand for about 15 minutes, until spongy.

Heat cream, milk and sugar in a saucepan over medium heat until just boiling. Remove from heat and add gelatine mixture and vanilla, stirring until gelatine has dissolved.

Pour mixture into six or eight ramekins. Refrigerate 6 hours (or overnight).

To serve, run a knife around the edge of each ramekin and unmould onto individual serving plates. Serve with fresh berries.

SERVES 6–8

Passionfruit custard

1½ cups castor sugar

4 eggs

1 cup cream

¾ cup passionfruit pulp

2 tablespoons lemon juice

Preheat oven to 160°C.

Whisk together 1 cup of the castor sugar, plus the eggs, cream, passionfruit and lemon juice.

Divide mixture between four 1-cup ramekins. Bake in a bain-marie (see page ix) for 25 minutes, or until set. Place ramekins on a wire rack to cool to room temperature. Then chill at least 4 hours before serving.

For topping, heat remaining sugar in a small saucepan over low heat until melted. Gently bring to the boil, then boil until it turns a dark golden colour. Pour over custard to cover. Cool at room temperature until toffee sets (do not refrigerate).

SERVES 4

Pavlova

4 egg whites

¼ teaspoon cream of tartar

1 cup castor sugar

2 teaspoons cornflour

1½ cups cream

fresh fruit (e.g. strawberries, raspberries,
  blueberries, kiwifruit, passionfruit pulp)

Preheat oven to 150°C. Line a baking tray with baking paper.

Beat the egg whites and cream of tartar in a clean, dry bowl until
stiff peaks form. Gradually beat in sugar until thick and glossy. Beat in
sifted cornflour.

Spoon mixture onto prepared tray and use a palette knife to shape it into
a circle about 3 cm high and flat on the top. Bake for about 1 hour, until
pale cream, risen and crisp. Cool on a wire rack.

To serve, top with whipped cream and decorate with fresh fruit.

SERVES 4–6

Peach and chocolate crumble

85 g unsalted butter

170 g plain flour

85 g soft brown sugar

4 peaches, stoned and diced

100 g milk or dark chocolate, chopped

Preheat oven to 180°C and grease a pie dish.

Blend the butter, sifted flour and sugar in a food processor until the mixture resembles fine breadcrumbs. Put crumble into a large bowl and mix in the peaches and chocolate.

Transfer mixture to the pie dish and bake for 12–14 minutes, until the crumble is golden, chocolate has melted and fruit is tender.

SERVES 4

Peach Melba

6 peaches

1½ cups white sugar

3 cups water

1 vanilla bean, split lengthways

300 g raspberries, fresh or frozen (defrosted)

¼ cup icing sugar

¼ cup water

Score a cross on the base of each peach. Gently heat white sugar, water and vanilla in a large saucepan until sugar has dissolved. Increase heat and bring to the boil. Add peaches and simmer for 5–10 minutes, until tender. Drain peaches and allow to cool, then remove skin.

For the sauce, purée raspberries, icing sugar and water in a blender. Push through a plastic sieve to remove seeds.

Serve each peach with a scoop of ice-cream and some raspberry purée drizzled over the top.

SERVES 6

Peanut butter brownies

BROWNIE

170 g unsalted butter

285 g dark cooking chocolate, chopped

1 cup castor sugar

1 teaspoon vanilla extract

pinch of salt

4 eggs

1 cup plain flour

1 cup roasted peanuts, chopped

TOPPING

1 cup crunchy peanut butter

100 g unsalted butter

½ cup icing sugar

1 tablespoon milk

150 g dark cooking chocolate, chopped

Preheat oven to 160°C. Grease and line a 30-cm × 23-cm shallow baking tin.

For brownie, melt butter and chocolate in a heavy-based saucepan over low heat until melted. Remove from heat and cool a little. Mix in sugar, vanilla and salt. Add eggs one at a time, mixing well after each addition. Gently fold in sifted flour, then fold in peanuts. Pour mixture into prepared tin and bake for 30 minutes, or until a skewer inserted comes out clean. Cool in the tin on a wire rack.

For topping, beat together peanut butter and half the butter until combined. Then beat in sifted icing sugar and milk. Spread mixture in an even layer over cooled brownie.

Melt remaining butter and chocolate in a heavy-based saucepan over low heat until melted and smooth. Carefully spread ganache evenly over peanut butter layer on brownies. Refrigerate at least 2 hours, until firm. Store in the refrigerator until 30 minutes before serving.

Cut into small squares or rectangles and serve at room temperature.

MAKES 40

Pear strudel

FILLING

60 g unsalted butter

4 pears, peeled, cored
  and chopped

1 teaspoon grated lemon zest

¼ cup brandy

⅓ cup soft brown sugar

1 tablespoon cornflour

½ teaspoon ground ginger

½ teaspoon ground cinnamon

¼ teaspoon ground nutmeg

PASTRY

9 sheets filo pastry

¾ cup finely crushed
  ginger-nut biscuits

100 g unsalted butter, melted

Preheat oven 190°C. Lightly grease a baking tray.

For filling, melt butter in a large frying pan. Add pears, lemon zest and brandy. Cook for about 10 minutes, until pears are tender. Stir in sugar, sifted cornflour and spices. Boil until sauce thickens. Set aside to cool.

Place one sheet of filo on a clean work surface. (Keep remaining filo covered with a damp tea towel so it doesn't dry out.) Brush filo sheet with melted butter, then place another sheet on top. Brush with butter and sprinkle with a tablespoon of the crushed biscuits. Repeat this process of layering filo, butter and biscuit crumbs with all but one of the remaining filo sheets. Top with the remaining filo sheet and brush with melted butter.

Spoon filling onto the filo, leaving a 5-cm border along the sides. Fold short sides over the filling and brush folded edges with melted butter. Beginning with a long side, carefully roll the strudel into a log to enclose the filling. Place strudel on prepared tray (seam side down), and brush with melted butter.

Bake 30 minutes, or until golden-brown. Dust with icing sugar.

Serve warm or at room temperature, with cream.

SERVES 6–8

Poached pears

4 pears, peeled, cored and sliced

200 ml white wine

200 g soft brown sugar

Place all ingredients into a frying pan and heat slowly, until sugar has dissolved.

Increase heat and bring to the boil. Simmer for about 10 minutes, until pears are soft.

Serve warm or cold, with the syrup.

SERVES 4

Poached quinces

2 cups castor sugar

2 litres water

6 quinces, peeled and halved

juice of 1 lemon

1 vanilla bean

1 cinnamon stick

2 cloves

Heat sugar and water over low heat until sugar has dissolved. Add the quinces, lemon juice and spices and simmer, covered, for about 4 hours, or until quinces are deep-red and tender.

Serve warm with cream.

SERVES 6

Quick apple tarts

1 sheet frozen puff pastry,
  thawed

3 golden delicious apples,
  peeled, cored, and thinly
  sliced

30 g unsalted butter, melted

3 tablespoons soft brown sugar

1 teaspoon ground cinnamon

¼ cup apricot jam

¼ cup raisins

Preheat oven to 200°C and line a baking tray with baking paper.

Cut pastry into six pieces and place on the baking tray. Use a fork
to prick holes all over the pastry. Arrange the apple slices on top,
overlapping, leaving a 5-mm border. Brush apples with melted butter.
Mix sugar and cinnamon together and sprinkle over apples.

Bake tarts for 30 minutes. Melt jam and brush over apples. Sprinkle
over raisins. Bake tart another 5–10 minutes, until golden.

Serve warm with vanilla ice-cream.

SERVES 6

Quick coconut rice pudding

2 cups cooked short-grain white rice, cold

2 cups milk

1½ cups coconut milk

⅓ cup castor sugar

pinch of salt

½ teaspoon vanilla extract

toasted coconut, to serve

pineapple and mango, to serve

Add rice, milk, coconut milk, sugar and salt to a heavy saucepan. Simmer uncovered for about 40 minutes, stirring frequently, until thickened. Stir in vanilla extract. Serve warm, garnished with toasted coconut and fruit.

SERVES 4

Raspberries with red wine

800 g fresh raspberries

100 g castor sugar

juice of 1 lemon

¼ cup red wine

1 tablespoon dry brandy

Gently toss raspberries with sugar and lemon juice. Set aside for at least an hour. Pour over the wine and brandy, cover and chill in the refrigerator for at least 2 hours, or overnight.

Serve with cream or ice-cream.

SERVES 6

Raspberry and apple crumble

FILLING

5 apples, peeled, cored
  and sliced

1 teaspoon ground cinnamon

1 teaspoon vanilla extract

2 tablespoons castor sugar

2 tablespoons water

300 g raspberries, fresh
  or frozen (defrosted)

CRUMBLE

100 g cold butter, cut into
  small pieces

¾ cup self-raising flour

¼ cup rolled oats

½ cup soft brown sugar,
  firmly packed

Preheat oven to 180°C and grease a baking dish.

For filling, put apple, cinnamon, vanilla, sugar and water into a saucepan. Cover and simmer until apples are just tender.

Pour mixture into baking dish and set aside to cool. When lukewarm, sprinkle over raspberries.

For crumble, rub butter into sifted flour until mixture resembles breadcrumbs. Mix in oats and sugar. Sprinkle topping over apples and raspberries.

Bake for 30 minutes or until golden brown.

Serve warm, with cream or custard.

SERVES 4–6

Raspberry coffee cake

CAKE

2 cups plain flour

2 teaspoons baking powder

½ teaspoon salt

60 g softened unsalted butter

½ cup castor sugar

1 egg

½ cup milk

200 g raspberries

TOPPING

⅓ cup plain flour

1 teaspoon ground cinnamon

½ cup castor sugar

60 g softened unsalted butter, chopped

Preheat oven to 190°C. Grease a 20-cm springform tin.

For cake, sift together flour, baking powder and salt.

In a separate bowl, cream butter and sugar until light and fluffy. Beat in the egg until combined. Add flour mixture a third at a time, alternating with the milk. Beat until smooth. Toss the berries in a little extra flour, then fold into the mixture. Pour into prepared tin.

For topping, sift flour and cinnamon into a bowl. Add sugar and butter and mix with a fork to make a crumbly mixture. Sprinkle evenly over cake batter.

Bake for 1 hour, or until a skewer inserted comes out clean.
Cool cake in the tin on a wire rack before turning out.

Serve with cream, as an accompaniment to coffee.

SERVES 6–8

Red wine jelly

2½ cups red wine

zest of 1 lemon

zest and juice of 1 orange

1 cinnamon stick

½ cup castor sugar

1 tablespoon gelatine

Stir wine, lemon and orange zest, cinnamon and sugar in a saucepan over low heat until sugar has dissolved. Simmer for 5 minutes then remove from the heat.

Pour orange juice into a small saucepan and sprinkle over gelatine. Set aside until soft and spongy, then heat gently until dissolved. Add to wine mixture.

Pour liquid through a fine sieve into a wet 3-cup jelly mould. Refrigerate for 3 hours or until set.

SERVES 4

Rhubarb cobbler

FILLING

1 kg rhubarb, trimmed
and diced

¼ cup soft brown sugar

1 teaspoon ground cinnamon

PASTRY

¼ cup castor sugar

2 cups plain flour

1 teaspoon baking powder

100 g cold butter, cut into
small pieces

⅓ cup milk

2 eggs, separated

Preheat oven to 200°C. Grease a 26-cm baking dish and chill.

For filling, toss rhubarb in brown sugar and cinnamon to coat.

For pastry, combine castor sugar, sifted flour and baking powder in
a bowl. Rub butter into flour mixture until it resembles breadcrumbs.

In a separate bowl, whisk together milk, 2 egg yolks and 1 egg white.
Add milk mixture to flour and mix to form a soft sticky dough.

Using half the mixture, spoon mounds of dough onto the base of the baking
dish and use well-floured hands to press it out to cover the base and sides.
Spoon rhubarb over the base. **>**

Cover rhubarb evenly with small spoonfuls of remaining dough. Brush top with remaining egg white.

Bake 30 minutes, or until golden. Cool in the dish on a wire rack.

Serve warm with cream or ice-cream.

SERVES 4 – 6

Rhubarb crumble

1 kg rhubarb, trimmed and cut into pieces

¾ cup castor sugar

100 g cold unsalted butter, cut into small pieces

¾ cup plain flour

⅓ cup soft brown sugar

12 sweet biscuits, crushed

Preheat oven to 200°C and grease a baking dish.

Place the rhubarb and castor sugar in a saucepan and heat gently until sugar has dissolved. Cover and simmer for 10 minutes, or until the rhubarb is tender. Transfer to baking dish.

For crumble, rub butter into sifted flour until mixture resembles breadcrumbs. Mix in soft brown sugar and crushed biscuits. Sprinkle crumble evenly over rhubarb.

Bake for 15 minutes, until golden-brown.

Serve hot with cream.

SERVES 8

Rich chocolate mousse

¾ cup white sugar

⅓ cup cocoa

3 tablespoons cornflour

¼ teaspoon salt

2 cups cream

85 g dark cooking chocolate,
   chopped

1 teaspoon vanilla extract

In a saucepan, mix together the sugar, and sifted cocoa, cornflour and salt.
Gradually mix in 1 cup of the cream. Once smooth, mix in remaining cream.
Bring to the boil over a medium heat and simmer until thick, about
5 minutes.

Remove from the heat and stir in chocolate and vanilla. Leave for
5 minutes, until chocolate has melted, then stir to just combine.

Pour into four ramekins or glasses. Refrigerate for at least 30 minutes
(or overnight). Serve with cream.

SERVES 4

Ricotta pancakes with banana

2 cups self-raising flour

⅓ cup castor sugar

200 g ricotta

1½ cups milk

2 egg whites

2 bananas, sliced, to serve

maple syrup and ice-cream,
to serve

Sift flour into a large bowl and add sugar. Beat in ricotta and milk.
In a separate bowl, beat egg whites until soft peaks form. Gently fold
egg whites into ricotta mixture.

Heat a frying pan over medium heat and brush with oil. When pan is hot,
pour in half a cup of mixture and tip pan until pancake is about 15 cm
across. Cook for about 2 minutes, until the surface of the pancake begins
to bubble (the underside should be golden-brown). Then flip the pancake
and cook the other side until golden.

Stack pancakes on a plate and keep warm while you finish cooking the
rest of the batter.

Serve with sliced banana, maple syrup and ice-cream.

SERVES 6–8

Roast figs in red wine

18 fresh figs

2½ cups red wine

1½ cups freshly squeezed orange juice

½ cup soft brown sugar

1 cup roasted walnuts, chopped

Preheat oven to 220°C.

Cut a cross into the top of each fig and squeeze gently so that the fig opens slightly at the top. Place in an ovenproof saucepan with the wine, orange juice and sugar. Bring to the boil and simmer for one minute.

Transfer to oven and bake for 8–10 minutes, until figs are cooked.

Serve immediately, sprinkled with walnuts.

SERVES 6

Roasted pears with caramel sauce

PEARS

100 g butter

2 pears, cored and halved

⅓ cup honey

SAUCE

2 tablespoons honey

⅓ cup water

2 tablespoons double cream

Preheat the oven to 200°C.

For the pears, melt the butter in an ovenproof frying pan. When the butter begins to foam, add the pear halves, flat-side down and fry for 5 minutes. Turn pear halves over, drizzle over honey, then place frying pan into the oven and bake for 5–10 minutes, until pears are tender.

For the caramel sauce, heat the honey and water in a saucepan. Once hot, stir in cream and simmer until thickened.

Pour sauce over pears, to serve.

SERVES 2

Sarah's cheesecake

1½ cups crushed arrowroot
    biscuits

100 g butter, melted

680 g cream cheese, at room
    temperature

1 cup white sugar

2 eggs

2 tablespoons freshly squeezed
    lemon juice

1 teaspoon vanilla extract

1 cup whipped cream

1 tablespoon castor sugar

1 teaspoon vanilla extract

ground cinnamon,
    for sprinkling

Preheat oven to 160°C and grease a 23-cm springform tin.

For base, mix together crushed biscuits and butter. Press mixture firmly into base of prepared tin. Wrap outside of the tin in three layers of foil. Refrigerate while making the filling.

For filling, beat cream cheese and sugar until smooth. Add eggs one at a time, beating after each addition until just blended. Add lemon juice and vanilla extract and beat until smooth.

Pour filling into tin. Bake in a bain-marie (see page ix) for 45 minutes, until edges have puffed up but centre is not completely set.

To make topping, beat cream, castor sugar and vanilla until stiff peaks form. Spread over cake and sprinkle with cinnamon.

Chill in the refrigerator overnight.

SERVES 12

Simple chocolate soufflé

140 g dark cooking chocolate, chopped

3 egg yolks

6 egg whites

pinch of salt

⅓ cup castor sugar

Preheat oven to 190°C. Grease a 6-cup soufflé dish and dust with castor sugar.

Melt chocolate (see page x). Cool a little, then stir in egg yolks. Set aside.

Beat egg whites with salt until soft peaks form. Gradually add sugar on medium speed, then beat at high speed until stiff peaks form. Fold a cup of the egg white mixture into the melted chocolate, then gently fold chocolate mixture into the egg white mixture until combined.

Pour mixture into prepared dish. Run a wet finger around the inside edge of the dish to help the soufflé rise evenly. Bake for 25 minutes, until puffed up and a crust has formed on top, but still a bit wobbly in the centre. Serve immediately.

SERVES 2–4

Spiced coffee cake

½ cup strong coffee, hot

4 cloves

2 cups self-raising flour

½ teaspoon ground nutmeg

1½ teaspoons ground cinnamon

½ teaspoon bicarbonate of soda

120 g softened butter

1 cup soft brown sugar

2 eggs, beaten

½ cup golden syrup

1 cup currants

1 cup sultanas

Soak cloves in coffee for at least 30 minutes.

Preheat oven to 180°C. Lightly grease a 20-cm cake tin.

Sift together flour, nutmeg, cinnamon and bicarbonate of soda.
In a separate bowl, cream butter and sugar until light and creamy.

Strain coffee to remove cloves. Add flour mixture to creamed mixture,
along with eggs, golden syrup and coffee. Beat until combined. Stir in
currants and sultanas.

Pour mixture into prepared tin and bake for 45 minutes, or until a skewer
inserted comes out clean.

SERVES 6-8

Spotted dick

1½ cups plain flour

1½ teaspoons baking powder

1 teaspoon ground cinnamon

½ cup castor sugar

2 cups fresh breadcrumbs

170 g sultanas, currants and
dried cherries

125 g vegetable suet, grated

1 teaspoon grated lemon zest

1 teaspoon grated orange zest

2 eggs

⅔ cup milk

Sift together flour, baking powder and cinnamon. Add sugar, breadcrumbs, dried fruit, suet and zest and mix well.

In a separate bowl, beat eggs and milk. Add to dry ingredients and mix well. (Add a little more milk if mixture is too dry.)

Transfer dough onto a sheet of baking paper. Roll into a log shape about 20-cm long. Loosely roll up dough in the baking paper. Wrap in a clean tea towel and steam for 1½ hours, topping up water as required.

Serve warm with custard or cream.

SERVES 6

Sticky date pudding

280 g pitted dates, chopped

2 cups water

1½ teaspoons bicarbonate
of soda

2 cups plain flour

½ teaspoon baking powder

1 teaspoon ground ginger

½ teaspoon salt

85 g softened unsalted butter

1 cup white sugar

3 eggs

SAUCE

200 g unsalted butter

1½ cups soft brown sugar,
firmly packed

1 cup thickened cream

½ teaspoon vanilla extract

Preheat oven to 190°C. Grease and flour a 20-cm square baking dish.

Simmer dates in the water for about 5 minutes. Remove from heat and stir in baking soda – the mixture will foam up. Let stand for 20 minutes.

Sift flour, baking powder, ginger and salt into a bowl. In a separate bowl, cream butter and sugar until light and fluffy. Add eggs one at a time, beating well after each addition. Add flour mixture in thirds, beating after each addition until just combined. Stir in date mixture until well combined.   >

Pour mixture into baking dish. Bake in a bain-marie (see page ix) for
35–40 minutes, or until a skewer inserted comes out clean. Cool in the
tin on a wire rack for 10 minutes.

To make sauce, melt butter then add sugar. Bring to the boil, stirring
occasionally, then stir in cream and vanilla. Simmer for about 5 minutes.

Serve pudding with warm sauce poured over, and ice-cream or cream
on the side.

SERVES 6–8

Strawberry tart

1½ cups plain flour

1½ teaspoons baking powder

pinch of salt

1 teaspoon ground cinnamon

80 g softened unsalted butter

¾ cup white sugar

2 eggs

2 tablespoons milk

1 teaspoon vanilla extract

500 g strawberries, hulled
and halved

Preheat oven to 180°C and grease a 20-cm springform tin.

Sift together flour, baking powder, salt and cinnamon.

In a separate bowl, cream the butter and the sugar until light and creamy.
Beat in the eggs, milk and vanilla. Stir the flour mixture into the creamed
mixture to just combine.

Pour into prepared tin. Arrange strawberry halves on top in a circular
pattern – push them down quite deeply into the dough. Bake for
30–35 minutes, or until a skewer inserted comes out clean.

Serve warm with cream.

SERVES 6–8

Summer pudding

20 slices white bread, crusts removed

1½ cups strawberries, hulled

4½ cups mixed berries, fresh or frozen

½ cup white sugar

¾ cup water

Preheat oven to 200°C.

Line a 6-cup bowl with the bread slices, overlapping them so that there are no gaps. Reserve a few slices to cover the top.

Put berries, sugar and water into a heavy-based saucepan. Stir over low heat for 5–10 minutes, until frozen berries have defrosted (if using) and sugar has dissolved.

Use a slotted spoon to transfer fruit into the bread-lined bowl. Cover with reserved bread. Pour over remaining liquid to soak bread. Place a weighted plate on top. Refrigerate overnight.

To serve, remove weighted plate and unmould pudding onto a serving platter. Serve with cream.

SERVES 6

Summer trifle

4 peaches, stoned and thinly
  sliced

700 g strawberries, hulled
  and halved

250 g raspberries

¼ cup white sugar

1 tablespoon Cointreau
  (or liqueur of choice)

3 cups thickened cream

1 tablespoon icing sugar

1 teaspoon vanilla extract

200 g sponge cake, sliced

1 cup strawberry or
  raspberry jam

Mix together fruit, sugar and liqueur. Let stand 10 minutes.

Whip the cream with sifted icing sugar and vanilla extract until stiff
peaks form.

Cover bottom of a 12-cup glass bowl (or individual glasses) with a third
of the sponge slices.

Spoon over a third of the jam. Cover with a third of the fruit mixture, then
a third of the whipped cream. Repeat with two more layers of sponge, jam,
fruit and cream.

Refrigerate for at least 2 hours before serving. Garnish with whole
strawberries, peach slices or grated chocolate.

SERVES 8–10

Sweet ricotta pie

1¾ cups plain flour

¼ cup white sugar

2 teaspoons grated orange zest

½ teaspoon salt

½ teaspoon baking powder

100 g cold unsalted butter, cut into small pieces

2 eggs

450 g ricotta

85 g cream cheese, at room temperature

1 tablespoon cornflour

1 teaspoon vanilla extract

¼ cup white sugar

2 eggs

2 teaspoons grated orange zest

Preheat oven to 180°C and grease a 24-cm loose-bottomed flan tin.

For the pastry, blend sifted flour, sugar, orange zest, salt and baking powder in a food processor. Add butter and blend until the mixture resembles coarse breadcrumbs. Add eggs and process until moist clumps form. Knead pastry on a well-floured board for about 1 minute. Divide into two pieces, with one piece slightly larger. Wrap the smaller piece in plastic film and store in the refrigerator. Use the larger piece to line the flan tin, covering the base and sides.

For the filling, beat together the ricotta, cream cheese, cornflour and vanilla. Beat in sugar, eggs and orange zest. >

Pour filling into pastry shell. Roll out remaining dough into a round piece 26 cm across. Place over filling and press edges into the sides of the tin to seal. Make three or four slits in the pastry.

Bake for about 1 hour, until golden. Cool in the tin on a wire rack.

SERVES 12

Tangy lemon curd mousse

10 egg yolks

1 cup white sugar

¾ cup freshly squeezed lemon juice

100 g unsalted butter

1 tablespoon grated lemon zest

1¼ cups thickened cream

Mix the egg yolks and sugar in a heavy-based saucepan. Add the lemon juice and butter and heat for about 5 minutes over a low heat, stirring constantly, until it just begins to simmer – do not boil.

Strain mixture through a sieve set over a bowl. Stir zest into sieved mixture, then cover with plastic film and set aside to cool. Once cool, transfer to refrigerator and chill for at least 4 hours (or overnight).

Beat the cream until stiff peaks form. Fold a third of the cream into the curd mixture until combined, then gently fold in remaining cream until combined.

Spoon mousse into individual serving bowls or glasses and chill, covered, for 6 hours before serving.

SERVES 8

Thai banana and coconut pudding

3 eggs

400 ml coconut milk

2 ripe bananas, chopped

¼ cup shredded coconut

2 tablespoons soft brown sugar

1 teaspoon vanilla extract

1 cup cooked vermicelli rice
noodles, cut into small pieces

toasted coconut, to serve

Preheat oven to 160°C. Lightly grease a small baking dish (with lid).

In a large bowl, whisk the eggs for about 1 minute, until light and fluffy. Add the coconut milk, bananas, shredded coconut, brown sugar and vanilla and mix well.

Add the noodles and stir to combine. Pour mixture into baking dish and cover. Bake for 1 hour, or until firm.

Serve with custard or ice-cream, with toasted coconut sprinkled on top.

SERVES 4–6

Tiramisu

500 g mascarpone

300 ml double cream

¾ cup espresso coffee

⅓ cup Amaretto or Tia Maria

18 sponge fingers

cocoa, to dust

Beat together the mascarpone and cream. Mix coffee and liqueur together. Dip sponge fingers into the coffee mixture. Put a layer of soaked sponge fingers into the bottom of a glass bowl or trifle dish. Add a layer of the mascarpone mixture. Repeat with one or two more layers of sponge and mascarpone mixture.

Refrigerate for at least 2 hours before serving. Dust with cocoa to serve.

SERVES 6

Toblerone pudding

PUDDING

1¼ cups plain flour

1 teaspoon baking powder

¼ cup cocoa

pinch of salt

1⅔ cups icing sugar

½ cup ground hazelnuts

70 g Toblerone chocolate, chopped

2 tablespoons unsalted butter, melted

1 egg

¾ cup milk

1 teaspoon vanilla extract

SAUCE

1 cup soft brown sugar

1¼ cups cocoa

2 cups boiling water

Preheat the oven to 180°C and grease a 30-cm shallow baking dish.

For the pudding, sift together the flour, baking powder, cocoa and salt. Add the sugar, ground hazelnuts and chocolate. In a separate bowl, beat the butter, egg, milk and vanilla. Stir egg mixture into flour mixture and mix thoroughly. Pour mixture into the prepared dish.

For the sauce, mix together the sugar and cocoa and sprinkle over the pudding mixture. Carefully pour the boiling water over the top. Bake for about 35 minutes, or until firm to the touch.

Serve hot, with cream.

SERVES 8

Tropical fruit salad

1 pineapple, peeled, cored and chopped

2 mangoes, peeled, stoned and sliced

2 bananas, peeled and sliced

¼ cup passionfruit pulp

¼ cup Malibu

¼ cup shredded coconut, toasted

Combine fruit and Malibu in a bowl, cover and refrigerate for 1 hour.

Toss through coconut and serve with whipped cream.

SERVES 4–6

Upside-down apricot pie

1 cup castor sugar

¼ cup water

1 tablespoon red-wine vinegar

1 × 400-g tin apricot halves,
  drained

2 tablespoons brandy

1 sheet frozen puff pastry

1 egg yolk

1 tablespoon milk

Heat sugar and water in a saucepan until sugar has dissolved. Boil until the syrup turns golden, then very carefully add the vinegar (it will spit). Stir until smooth, then pour into a greased 25-cm pie dish, coating the base.

Toss the fruit with the brandy and place in the dish. Cover the fruit with the pastry, pressing the pastry firmly against the edges of the pie dish. Refrigerate for 20 minutes.

Preheat oven to 200°C.

Mix the egg yolk and milk together and brush over the pastry. Bake for around 30 minutes or until the top is brown.

Run a knife around the edge of the pie dish and carefully turn the pie over onto a serving plate.

Serve hot, with cream or ice-cream.

SERVES 6

Vodka raspberry jelly

300 g raspberries, fresh or frozen (defrosted)

¾ cup castor sugar

¼ cup vodka

1 litre water

3 tablespoons gelatine

Stir raspberries, sugar, vodka and water in a saucepan over low heat until sugar has dissolved. Cover and bring to the boil, then simmer for 15 minutes. Remove from heat and set aside to cool for 15 minutes.

Push mixture through a fine sieve to remove seeds. Pour a little of the syrup into a small saucepan and sprinkle over the gelatine. Set aside until soft and spongy, then heat gently until dissolved. Add to remaining syrup.

Pour the mixture into a wet 1.25-litre jelly mould, or 8 individual glasses or moulds, and refrigerate for 4 hours, or until set.

SERVES 8

Walnut brownies

200 g dark cooking chocolate,
   chopped

175 g softened unsalted butter

2 eggs

1 cup soft brown sugar

1 cup plain flour

3 tablespoons cocoa

100 g toasted walnuts, chopped

icing sugar, to dust

Preheat oven to 160°C. Grease and line a 23-cm cake tin.

Melt chocolate and butter in a double boiler or in the microwave
(see page x). Set aside to cool.

Beat eggs and sugar until thick and creamy. Fold in melted chocolate,
then stir in sifted flour and cocoa. Finally fold in walnuts.

Pour mixture into cake tin. Bake for 30 minutes, or until just firm
to the touch. (Brownies will become more solid as they cool.)

Once cool, dust with icing sugar and cut into squares.

MAKES ABOUT 24

White chocolate and orange soufflé

½ cup thickened cream

¼ cup white sugar

230 g good quality white chocolate, chopped

4 egg yolks

2 teaspoons grated orange zest

1 tablespoon Grand Marnier

3 egg whites

2 tablespoons icing sugar

extra icing sugar, to dust

Preheat oven to 180°C. Grease a 6-cup soufflé dish and dust with castor sugar.

Stir together cream and white sugar in a heavy-based saucepan until sugar dissolves. Add 170 g of the chocolate and heat gently until chocolate has melted. Mix in egg yolks and orange zest. Heat for about 5 minutes, stirring constantly, until mixture thickens a little – do not boil. Mix in Grand Marnier. Pour into a bowl and set aside to cool.

Beat egg whites until soft peaks form. Add icing sugar and beat until stiff peaks form. Mix remaining chocolate into the warm egg yolk mixture and stir until chocolate has almost melted. Fold in half the egg whites until combined, then gradually fold in remaining egg whites.

Pour mixture into prepared soufflé dish. Bake for about 35 minutes, until puffed up and golden brown.

Dust with icing sugar to serve.

SERVES 6

Zuppa inglese

2 cups milk

2 teaspoons vanilla extract

4 egg yolks

½ cup castor sugar

2 tablespoons plain flour

300 g sponge cake, cut into 1-cm thick slices

⅓ cup dark rum

grated chocolate or slivered almonds, to serve

Slowly heat milk and vanilla until hot but not boiling. In a bowl, whisk together egg yolks, sugar and sifted flour.

Gradually whisk the hot milk into the egg mixture until well combined. Pour into a clean saucepan and heat, stirring constantly, until boiling and thickened.

Line the base of a serving dish (or individual glasses) with slices of sponge cake. Brush the sponge slices with rum, then pour over a third of the custard mixture. Repeat this process – adding layers of sponge, rum and custard – twice more, finishing with a layer of custard. Cover with plastic film and chill for at least 3 hours.

Decorate with grated chocolate or slivered almonds to serve.

SERVES 4–6

Conversions

LIQUIDS

Millilitres	Fluid ounces
60 ml	2 fl oz
125 ml	4 fl oz
200 ml	6 fl oz
250 ml	8 fl oz
500 ml	16 fl oz
625 ml	20 fl oz (1 pint)

WEIGHTS

Grams	Ounces
30 g	1 oz
60 g	2 oz
90 g	3 oz
125 g	4 oz
250 g	8 oz
375 g	12 oz
500 g	16 oz (1 lb)
1 kg	2 lb

OVEN TEMPERATURES

Celsius	Fahrenheit
150	300
180	360
190	375
200–230	400–450
250–260	475–500

CAKE TIN SIZES

Centimetres	Inches
6 cm	2.5 in
7 cm	3 in
15 cm	6 in
18 cm	7 in
20 cm	8 in
23 cm	9 in
24 cm	9.5 in
25 cm	10 in
30 cm	12 in
33 cm	13 in
38 cm	15 in

Index

PENGUIN BOOKS

Published by the Penguin Group
Penguin Group (Australia)
250 Camberwell Road, Camberwell, Victoria 3124, Australia
(a division of Pearson Australia Group Pty Ltd)
Penguin Group (USA) Inc.
375 Hudson Street, New York, New York 10014, USA
Penguin Group (Canada)
90 Eglinton Avenue East, Suite 700, Toronto ON M4P 2Y3, Canada
(a division of Pearson Penguin Canada Inc.)
Penguin Books Ltd
80 Strand, London WC2R 0RL, England
Penguin Ireland
25 St Stephen's Green, Dublin 2, Ireland
(a division of Penguin Books Ltd)
Penguin Books India Pvt Ltd
11 Community Centre, Panchsheel Park, New Delhi – 110 017, India
Penguin Group (NZ)
67 Apollo Drive, Rosedale, North Shore 0632, New Zealand
(a division of Pearson New Zealand Ltd)
Penguin Books (South Africa) (Pty) Ltd
24 Sturdee Avenue, Rosebank, Johannesburg 2196, South Africa

Penguin Books Ltd, Registered Offices: 80 Strand, London, WC2R 0RL, England

First published by Penguin Group (Australia), 2007

10 9 8 7 6 5 4 3

Many thanks to Freedom Furniture South Yarra, Dinosaur Designs, and Matchbox in Armadale
for their lovely range of props.

Design by Claire Tice © Penguin Group (Australia)
Photography by Julie Renouf
Food styling by Linda Brushfield
Typeset by Post Pre-press Group, Brisbane, Queensland
Colour separations by Splitting Image P/L, Clayton
Printed in China by Everbest Printing Co. Ltd

National Library of Australia
Cataloguing-in-Publication data:

Dessert bible.
Includes index.
ISBN 978 0 14 300645 9 (pbk.).
1. Desserts. 2. Cookery (Puddings).

641.86